THE GOOD, THE BAD, AND THE UGLY
PHILADELPHIA EAGLES

HEART-POUNDING, JAW-DROPPING, AND GUT-WRENCHING
MOMENTS FROM PHILADELPHIA EAGLES HISTORY

Steve Silverman

TRIUMPH
BOOKS

Triumph Books and colophon are registered trademarks of
Random House, Inc.

Library of Congress Cataloging-in-Publication Data

Silverman, Steve, 1956–
   The good, the bad, and the ugly Philadelphia Eagles: heart-pound-
ing, jaw-dropping, and gut-wrenching moments from Philadelphia
Eagles history / Steve Silverman.
       p. cm.
   Includes bibliographical references.
   ISBN-13: 978-1-57243-989-4
   ISBN-10: 1-57243-989-0
   1. Philadelphia Eagles (Football team)—History. I. Title.
GV956.P44S55 2008
796.332'640974811—dc22
                                                2008021090

This book is available in quantity at special discounts for your group
or organization. For further information, contact:

Triumph Books
542 South Dearborn Street
Suite 750
Chicago, Illinois 60605
(312) 939-3330
Fax (312) 663-3557

Printed in U.S.A.
ISBN: 978-1-57243-989-4
All photos courtesy of AP Images unless unless
otherwise indicated.

Content packaged by Mojo Media, Inc.
Joe Funk: Editor
Jason Hinman: Creative Director

Design by Patricia Frey

The journey is not always an easy one. I dedicate this book to Samantha and Gregory, who are always with me every step of the way. I also want to remember my mother, Gloria, who had a love of writing and a way with words. She always knew how to say the right thing.

CONTENTS

PREFACE

I had my lightbulb moment when I was seven years old. One moment I was playing with a toy truck in the family room of my house, oblivious to what was going on in the world outside my neighborhood. The next minute I was watching Mickey Mantle hit a game-winning home run in the 1964 World Series (in Game 3 versus the Cardinals off knuckleballer Barney Schultz). From that moment on, sports became the most important thing in my life.

Like many of you, I had dreams of becoming a professional athlete; however, reality grabbed me around the throat by the time seventh grade was over. I was a pretty good ballplayer, but there were dozens better in my hometown of Cranford, New Jersey, a township that does not have a long history of producing major league athletes.

I ate up *The* (Newark) *Star-Ledger's* sports section every morning, and when I realized that you could get paid for going to baseball, football, and hockey games and writing about them, my path was obvious.

Little has changed except that my love for the Yankees reversed 180 degrees and I became a Red Sox fan. The story on how that happened would take too long to tell, but the Red Sox's heroic performance in losing the 1975 World Series to the Cincinnati Reds was basically where it started.

As I got involved in the business, covering pro football became my career of choice. There is no better sport to cover; it has brought me in touch with great people at every level of the game.

One of those great individuals was the late New York Giants owner Wellington Mara, who sent me several handwritten letters while I was a writer and editor at *Pro Football Weekly* from 1986 to 1996. His letters conveyed his constant interest in bettering the game; it's the same reason he chose to support sharing television revenues equally with his fellow owners, instead of hoarding the largest share for the Giants (who reside in New York, the league's biggest market, and therefore stood to make the most money from broadcast revenues). He knew that sharing the revenues equally would help every member of the league to grow, and that that would help his team more in the long run than any immediate financial gain.

As much as he wanted to help other teams to grow, Mara also enjoyed his team's rivalries with organizations like the Redskins, the Cowboys, and particularly the Eagles. The four core members of the NFC East have shared many memorable games over the years, but none of their rivals have inspired more passion than the Eagles, whose fans don't just support their team, but also know how to run it.

The same couldn't always be said for late owner Leonard Tose, who had many problems that ultimately ruined his life. Still, he gets the credit for hiring Dick Vermeil, a head coach who changed a losing culture into a winning one. During his first season in Philadelphia, Vermeil held open tryouts for anyone who thought they might be able to help the Eagles. The unusual move brought out players of every shape and size—and it sent a message to his players. It told them that their new coach would do anything he could to bring talent to the roster. The tryout produced an unlikely star in Vince Papale, whose story was turned into a movie in 2006. It also got the franchise moving in the right direction.

Since the arrival of Vermeil, the Eagles have been one of the league's most fascinating teams, with players like Reggie White, Ron Jaworski, Wilbert Montgomery, Bill Bergey, Randall Cunningham, Mike Quick, Eric Allen, Donovan McNabb, and yes, Terrell Owens.

After Vermeil, the coaches have run the gamut from the

calm, cool, and carefully thought-out persona of Andy Reid to the passion and emotion of Buddy Ryan and the dunderheadedness of Rich Kotite.

The Eagles, of course, had a long history before Vermeil came on the scene. Bert Bell's original Eagles needed time to learn to fly, but the championship teams of 1948 and 1949 had perhaps the game's best running back in Steve Van Buren and the league's toughest player in Chuck Bednarik—otherwise known as "Concrete Charlie"—who won those two championships early in his career and then capped his playing days by winning the 1960 NFL Championship over the Green Bay Packers. That game was to be the only postseason defeat that Vince Lombardi would ever suffer, and Bednarik made the deciding play when he tackled fullback Jim Taylor and would not let him up until the final gun.

Eagles fans have been waiting, hoping, and praying for another championship team since then. Two Super Bowl visits have ended in pain, but the spirit of the most loyal, passionate, and knowledgeable fans in sports has endured for generations and shows no signs of abating.

INTRODUCTION

The Philadelphia Eagles have run the gamut in the NFL. Under the leadership of owner Jeff Lurie and head coach Andy Reid, they have been among the most consistent teams in the league; they have also had some of the saddest teams in the history of the game.

Who can forget the sorrowful ownership of men like Jerry Wolman, Leonard Tose, and Norman Braman? Coaches Joe Kuharich, Rich Kotite, and Ed "The Hatchet" Khayat are among the biggest losers the game has ever seen.

Eagles fans have been hardened by what they have had to endure over the years. They are tough, discerning, and demanding. They have seen more than their share of defeats stolen from the jaws of victory over the years. It is no wonder that a misshapen Santa Claus was once booed and pelted with snowballs by angry Eagles fans.

Tose is one of the most pivotal men in team history, and his impact on the NFL should serve as a cautionary tale. Viewed as a savior when he purchased the team from the bumbling Jerry Wolman, he made the hire of a lifetime when he brought Dick Vermeil in from UCLA to coach the Eagles in 1976. Tose didn't know Vermeil. He had merely watched UCLA upset Woody Hayes and Ohio State in the Rose Bowl on New Year's Day. Tose was impressed with the 23–10 win, but what really got to him was Vermeil's star power. He sensed it watching the game on television;

he thought Vermeil would have the fire to turn the franchise around. That was one bet that Tose won—big time. Vermeil led the Eagles on a path to greatness that would see them beat the Dallas Cowboys in the 1980 NFC Championship Game before losing Super Bowl XV to the Oakland Raiders.

When Vermeil arrived in Philadelphia, the team lacked quality personnel and the conditioning was abysmal. Vermeil would change both of those situations dramatically. He traded for a relative unknown, Ron Jaworski, who would prove to be a great quarterback, and he drafted one of the league's top running backs in Wilbert Montgomery. With a defense led by nasty linebackers Bill Bergey and Jerry Robinson, along with a hard-hitting secondary that included Herman Edwards and Randy Logan, the Eagles quickly became one of the NFL's best teams.

But after Vermeil left following the strike-torn 1982 season, Philadelphia's fortunes went downhill. There were struggles on the field under Marion Campbell, but "The Swamp Fox" wasn't necessarily to blame. Tose was in the grip of a gambling addiction that would decimate his fortune and destroy his life.

Despite the team's many ups and downs, Eagles fans have always followed their team with scrutiny, passion, and love. The fans know that winning every year is not possible, but they want a front office, a coaching staff, and a team that cares about the game as much as they do. This is not a group of fans that will accept stumblebums, double-talkers, or fools. That's why men like Kuharich, Khayat, and Kotite had no chance.

The Eagles have enjoyed a period of sustained success under Lurie and Reid. They have a top quarterback in Donovan McNabb and a defense that has been among the league's best. They made it to Super Bowl XXXIX following the 2004 season, but once again fell short of a championship. The 24–21 loss to the Patriots could easily have gone the other way; McNabb and a one-year stud in Terrell Owens nearly got the team to the promised land.

The Eagles continue to fight the good fight, and their fans continue to back them. But that doesn't mean they will blindly accept whatever is put on their plate. Eagles fans are probably the most demanding and knowledgeable in the NFL. Close is not good enough for them; there will be no letup until this team can repeat what happened in 1960. That was the last year the Eagles won the NFL championship. Head coach Buck Shaw let his players have fun, Norm Van Brocklin was a good passer and a great leader, and Chuck Bednarik was the most feared player in the league. That team gave the legendary Vince Lombardi his only postseason defeat as a head coach, and it is the kind of performance Eagles fans are aching to see once again.

THE EARLY YEARS

BERT BELL AND THE ORIGIN OF THE EAGLES

From humble beginnings did the Eagles take wing.

The Frankford Yellow Jackets, the city's first professional football team, played their last game in 1931, after which they filed for bankruptcy and went out of business. It was a fate suffered by many businesses in Philadelphia—and throughout the country—as the nation struggled through the height of the Great Depression.

But just because that team had withered away didn't mean that there was no interest in pro football in the city. Philadelphia's football future was saved by DeBenneville "Bert" Bell in 1933. The man who would eventually become one of the game's great innovators wanted to bring football back to Philadelphia. Growing up in one of the richest families in Philadelphia, he went on to play college football at Penn (as a 150-pound quarterback). He loved the game despite his upper-crust upbringing.

Bell later coached at both Penn and Temple. He got involved with the professional game when he formed a syndicate with former Penn teammate Lud Wray to buy the Yellow Jackets for $2,500 in 1933. The two also agreed to guarantee the debts the team owed to the Chicago Bears, the New York Giants, and the Green Bay Packers. Bell's first act as owner was to rename the team, and the Philadelphia Eagles were in business.

Wray had been recommended to Boston Redskins owner George

Preston Marshall as a head coach by Bell the previous year, and he had coached that team to a 4–4–2 record. He left the Redskins after that season to take over the sideline duties for the Eagles.

An early highlight for the Eagles came not on the field but at the negotiating table. Pennsylvania blue laws at that time strictly forbid holding sporting events on Sundays. Bell was able to overcome those arcane laws, receiving a license to play on Sundays—which, as everyone knows, have since become *the* day for professional football.

Sadly, the Eagles had limited talent on the field, dropping their first three games before recording a road win over the Cincinnati Reds. They came home to face the defending league champion Chicago Bears; the Eagles held George Halas's team to a 3–3 tie.

It would be a long time before the Eagles would become respectable on the field or profitable at the box office. The low point may have come during the 1939 season, when the Eagles played a scoreless tie against the Brooklyn Dodgers at Municipal Stadium in a driving rainstorm before less than 100 fans.

Bell became the coach and sole owner of the team in 1936. He coached the team unsuccessfully for five years before a very strange business deal took place. In 1940 Art Rooney, owner of the Pittsburgh Steelers (then known as the Pirates), sold his franchise to Alexis Thompson; Rooney then became Bell's partner in Philadelphia. The two teams then traded locations: Thompson took the original version of the Steelers to Philadelphia and the Bell-Rooney coalition went to Pittsburgh with the Eagles.

The Eagles, merged with the Pittsburgh team, continued to struggle through the 1942 season. The 1943 season was nearly suspended because so many of the players had left the league to take up military service during World War II. But the league soldiered on. Since there weren't enough players, the Eagles and the Steelers decided to combine to become the "Steagles" for one season. The combined team went 5–4–1, marking the first time the Eagles—in any form—had a winning season.

The two teams separated the following year; the Eagles resumed playing on their own while Bell's Steelers merged with the Cardinals. The Eagles became a football power in 1944 with a 7–1–2

Bert Bell, right, President of the Philadelphia Eagles pro football club, presents Texas Christian All-American back Davey O'Brien with the Maxwell Award as the Outstanding College Player of 1938 in Philadelphia on January 10, 1939.

record and a second-place finish, while the Card-Pitts went 0–10.

Bell escaped the ongoing mess of professional football in the area two years later when he agreed to succeed Elmer Layden as commissioner of the league. Not only was Bell charged with leading the league in the postwar era, he also had to deal with the heavy hand of George Halas in Chicago. Halas was one of the founders of the NFL and had had a hand in nearly every decision the league made. While Bell had a vision that would take the league into the future, Halas tended to focus only on how each issue would impact his own team. However, Halas recognized Bell's strengths and Bell realized that he needed to get along with Halas. The two did just enough compromising to allow the league to move forward.

Bell endorsed the creation of a players association, a group that would eventually become the National Football League Player's

Association (NFLPA). NFL owners were aghast that the commissioner would help the players unionize, but Bell thought it was the right thing to do, since the league was being built on the players' backs. He also instituted the league's first pension plan. And it was Bell who negotiated the merger with the All-American Football Conference (AAFC), an agreement that ended the war between the two leagues and brought the Cleveland Browns, the San Francisco 49ers, and the Baltimore Colts into the NFL.

Bell came up with the concept of sudden death overtime for playoff games, a rule that became reality in perhaps the most important game in pro football history when the Colts defeated the Giants 23–17 in the 1958 NFL Championship game. That overtime contest transfixed a nation of fans—including Lamar Hunt, who was also destined to become an important figure in the history of pro football.

In 1959 the 26-year-old Hunt, son of oil magnate H.L. Hunt, was far more interested in owning a football team than he was in pumping oil. But the NFL rebuffed Hunt at every turn, denying him both an expansion franchise and an existing one. So Hunt decided to start his own league—the American Football League (AFL).

Surprisingly, Hunt received some of his strongest encouragement and his best advice from Bell. Even though he was commissioner of the NFL, Bell thought his league had its strongest growth period when it was competing with and then eventually merged with the AAFC. Bell believed that Hunt's new league, if it could get off the ground, would create more interest in the game of professional football among the fans and the media, something that would help both organizations.

Bell's thinking about the AFL turned out to be prophetic. The new league eventually became one of the biggest success stories in the history of pro football—but sadly Bell was not around to enjoy a congratulatory hug from Hunt. Bert Bell died when he suffered a heart attack on October 12, 1959, while watching the Eagles play the Steelers at Franklin Field. He was 65 years old.

Bell's death scuttled his secret plan to reacquire the Eagles. He had planned to step down from the commissioner's office and then buy the Eagles just three days later for $900,000. He had told no one of his plan except for his son, Bert Jr.

Bell's vision, decisiveness, and ability to grow a product have led to quite a legacy—the most successful professional sporting league in the world. And while the venerable Halas may have been the backbone of the league, Bell was clearly its conscience.

HITTING THAT CHAMPIONSHIP STRIDE

The majority of football fans can easily identify the best defensive teams in NFL history. The legendary Steel Curtain under Steelers head coach Chuck Noll is often viewed as the best defensive team of all time. The rowdy 1985 Chicago Bears come within a hair of those Steelers, with Don Shula's undefeated Dolphins right behind them. Vince Lombardi's Packers, the Purple People Eaters of Minnesota, and the Rams' Fearsome Foursome must also be taken into consideration.

The 1948–49 Philadelphia Eagles may not be as well known as those teams, but they were probably just as good on the field. Head coach Earle "Greasy" Neale was the top defensive of his time, putting together an inventive five-man defensive line that featured two added linebackers and four defensive backs. The group was led by Frank "Bucko" Kilroy, Alex Wojciechowicz, Vic Sears, and eventually Chuck Bednarik—a group of defenders who inflicted punishment on nearly every play.

Opponents complained that the Eagles were dirty, claiming that Kilroy was particularly nasty. He was even featured in a *Life* magazine profile on professional football entitled "Savagery on Sunday." The story portrayed Kilroy, who would go on to become a longtime executive with the New England Patriots, as one of the "bad guys" of the game.

Kilroy did not take these accusations of dirty play lightly. He fought in the trenches on both sides of the Philadelphia line and didn't admit to anything except playing hard. He resented what was said and written about him. "That is the reply of losers," he said. "The losers will never admit that the Eagles were just the more physical team, or that the Eagles just wanted it more. The losers will not state, 'Wow! The Eagles physically blew us off the

THE FIRST NFL DRAFT

It is as big an off-season event as there is in the world of professional sports. When the NFL gets together in late April to draft the new class of rookies, everybody watches. The event is televised from start to finish, and analysis of the players has become a significant industry in itself.

To say that the NFL Draft has grown over the years is putting it mildly. It has become a huge media event that also has major significance when it comes to building talent within an organization.

Bell came up with the idea for the draft in 1935 and sold his fellow owners on the concept; it was soon embraced throughout the league. He was tired of seeing teams like the Giants and the Bears dominate the league. He wanted his team—as well as the rest of the league—to have a legitimate chance to improve their rosters. Under Bell's new system, teams would select players with whom they would then have exclusive negotiating rights; the teams with the poorest records would select first.

Bell thought George Halas might object to the idea, since his team was already winning (and making money) without the draft. But when Halas realized that the draft would save him money because he wouldn't have to outbid his competition, he quickly fell in line.

The first draft was held in Philadelphia in 1936, and the Eagles had the first pick as a result of their abysmal 2–9 record the previous season. The best player in college football in 1935 was Jay Berwanger, a running back from the University of Chicago's Maroons, who were a major power in the Big Ten at that time. (Football would eventually lose its importance at the institution, and the school dropped the sport. They later brought it back at the Division III level.) Berwanger had said that he had no interest in playing pro football, but the Eagles drafted him anyway. They traded his rights to the Bears before the end of the draft, but Berwanger decided not to turn pro and never played in the NFL.

The Boston Redskins took Alabama's Riley Smith with the second pick, and he signed. Smith wasn't hoping to get rich by playing in the NFL; he just wanted to continue playing. "I signed because I wasn't ready to quit playing ball," Smith told Bob Barnett of the Professional Football Researchers Association (PFRA). "I just wanted to keep playing. I signed for $250 a game and a little bonus. We won the Eastern Division Championship twice and the NFL Championship once in the three years I played, and the most I ever got was $350 a game. I made more money in the off-season. I quit in 1938 and took a coaching job at Washington and Lee [University] for a lot more money. But we had it good, because some of those fellas down in Philadelphia were playing for $60 and $70 a ballgame."

Bell's little innovation has become the lifeblood of the NFL and a major media event. Mel Kiper and all the draftniks should say a little prayer of thanks to Saint Bert on Draft Eve every year.

line of scrimmage running [Steve] Van Buren down our throats!'" The Eagles relied on Van Buren for both offense and their nasty defense.

This dominating Philadelphia squad shut out the Chicago Cardinals 7–0 in the 1948 NFL Championship and then blanked the Los Angeles Rams 14–0 in the following year's NFL Championship. No team in NFL history before or since had reeled off shutouts in consecutive NFL Championship games.

"Being a member of back-to-back championship teams was a great feeling! But to be a part of a defense that posted back-to-back championship shutouts is very special," recalled Kilroy.

Kilroy's nasty style forced a fumble in the game versus the Cardinals, and the Eagles recovered the loose ball. That play led to the game's only touchdown, a five-yard run by Van Buren. Kilroy's tough play allowed the Eagles to limit the Cardinals to just six total first downs. "Defensively, coming hard off the ball, I just took a crease and found myself in the backfield. I think it disrupted the running back, and I stripped him of the ball," Kilroy told writer Gary Kravitz.

Neale was a thinking man's coach. Gruff in language and tough in appearance, he knew that the late 1940s were a changing era in the nation as a whole and in professional sports in particular. Many of the Eagles' players were returning World War II veterans, so Neale thought it unnecessary to take the tough disciplinary approach many coaches favored. He reasoned that four years of participation in the war effort entitled the players to be treated like men instead of schoolchildren. He allowed them to tease and kid him, although they never crossed the line with behavior that would have impeded his authority. Neale also valued his players' opinions, inspiring a great deal of love among them. He treated men like men—and even sought out their advice on things like play calling. Neale reasoned that his players were intelligent "college men," and he recognized that they were in a perfect position to see who might be the opponent's weak point and where to focus the team's attack.

The Eagles could have achieved three consecutive championships if they had beaten the Cardinals in the 1947 championship game. The game was played on a blisteringly cold day on a frozen Comiskey Park field. The Cardinals had covered their field with a tarp all week, but 24 hours before the game the ground crew took it off so the Cardinals wouldn't have to pay them extra to come and do it on the weekend.

By the time the game began the ground was more like a sheet of ice than a football field. The Cardinals came out wearing gym shoes with cork cleats, while the Eagles put on their regular spikes, filed down to keep them from getting stuck in the ice. But the officials ruled that those shoes were not safe, so the Eagles changed to regular sneakers—but without the cork the Cardinals had. That disadvantage, combined with the cold, virtually killed the Eagles running game; Van Buren was held to just 26 yards.

Despite the conditions, the Eagles fought valiantly. The passing game was particularly effective: unheralded quarterback Tommy Thompson completed 27 of 44 passes for 297 yards and a touchdown. The Eagles also outgained the Cardinals (357 yards to Chicago's 336) and controlled the ball, gaining 22 first downs to Chicago's 11. But with Van Buren's performance compromised, the team struggled, finally losing 28–21.

Philadelphia got its revenge—and the first half of its two-year championship run—the next season. They were hard-hitting, nasty, and played with a purpose. Nobody ever mentions this team's name among the NFL's greatest, but back-to-back championship game shutouts speak for themselves. This team was a true gem.

TOP CLUTCH PERFORMERS

CONCRETE CHARLIE

In a sport filled with fearless warriors, Chuck Bednarik stands out as one of the toughest guys to ever play the game.

The list of the roughest football players ever—while open to much debate—also includes Doug Atkins, Dick Butkus, Joe Greene, Charles Haley, Dan Hampton, Deacon Jones, Jack Lambert, Ray Lewis, "Big Daddy" Lipscomb, Gino Marchetti, Lawrence Taylor, Randy White, and Jack Youngblood. This author's bet is that if you put them all in a room, Bednarik, Butkus, or Taylor would be the only one to walk out again.

Legendary running back Jim Brown, perhaps the greatest football player of all time, is a man of immense pride. He has walked with the titans of the sports world, as well as the stars of Hollywood. "Chuck Bednarik was as great as any linebacker who has ever lived," Brown said. "I don't know how old he is, but I'll bet nobody could kick his butt today."

Bednarik was born in 1925. He was 79 when Brown made his assessment.

Bednarik played center on offense and middle linebacker on defense for the Eagles. He grew up in Bethlehem, Pennsylvania, played college football at Penn, and had a 14-year career with the Eagles, from 1949 to 1962. He was one of the last of the two-way players and was often called "The 60-Minute Man," although that was a slight exaggeration. Bednarik played every snap on offense and every snap on defense, but he was on the sideline for kickoffs.

But in the 1960 NFL Championship game, he was on the field for more than 58 actual game minutes.

"Concrete Charlie" was a warrior who earned his spot in the Hall of Fame alongside legends like George Halas and Vince Lombardi. He is best known for two legendary plays: a knockout hit on Frank Gifford during the Eagles' 1960 championship season and a last-second tackle of Jim Taylor that preserved the Eagles' win over the Packers in that season's title game.

The repercussions of the Gifford hit have been reverberating through the NFL for decades. With the Eagles leading the Giants 17–10 at Yankee Stadium in the fourth quarter of their battle for first place in the Eastern Conference, New York had the ball and was driving for the tying touchdown. Giants quarterback Charley Conerly hit Gifford with a pass over the middle, but before he could make a move upfield, he was met head-on by Bednarik. The full-speed hit sent Gifford flying backward, his head hitting the frozen turf and his arms and legs splaying back. Gifford did not move.

The great stadium went silent. Everyone who witnessed that moment shared the eerie feeling that something awful had happened to Gifford.

"I knew I did a lot of damage as soon as I hit him," Bednarik said. "It was like a truck hitting a Volkswagen. Frank never saw me or heard me until it was too late."

The force of the collision shocked teammates—men who made their living obliterating opposing ball carriers. "I played the game a long time, but I never heard a sound on the football field anything close to that hit," said Tom Brookshier, an Eagles defensive back and a longtime partner of Pat Summerall on CBS's NFL broadcasts. "It wasn't the usual kind of thud that you hear on a big hit. It was a loud crack. Think about an ax hitting dry wood. I saw Frank on the ground and he looked like a corpse. I thought he was dead."

Thankfully, Gifford was still breathing and suffered no permanent damage. But he did take the 1961 season off before returning for three more seasons in 1962. Gifford would later become a longtime *Monday Night Football* announcer.

But back in 1960, things looked much grimmer. As the ball

rolled away from the unconscious running back, Eagles middle linebacker Chuck Weber rolled on the ball and recovered. A *Sports Illustrated* photo published at the time seemed to show Bednarik celebrating the damage he had done to Gifford, but he was merely reacting to his team's recovery of the ball and the fact that it ensured victory.

"I said, 'This f---ing game is over,'" Bednarik said. "I wasn't directing it at Frank. I was just happy we won. If people think I was gloating over Frank, they couldn't have been more wrong." Nevertheless, that play symbolized what Bednarik was all about and the standard that he set. The Eagles went on to win the Eastern Conference title, earning the right to meet the up-and-coming Green Bay Packers and Vince Lombardi.

Even though the game was played in Philadelphia, most experts expected the Packers to win. Green Bay had Bart Starr, Paul Hornung, Jim Taylor, Willie Davis, and, of course, Vince Lombardi prowling the sideline. The Eagles had Norm Van Brocklin and Bednarik, both of whom were aging by that time, and a slew of role players.

The Eagles played with passion and guts, holding a 17–13 lead in the closing seconds. But it was Green Bay that held the ball at the Philadelphia 22-yard line when there was time for just one more play. Starr could not find an open receiver in the end zone, so he dumped the ball off to Taylor, a concrete block of a man who lowered his head and powered his way to the 9-yard line. Bednarik was right there to meet him. He stopped Taylor, got him to the ground, and did not get off of him until the game was over.

"Taylor was moving and squirming, trying to get up," Bednarik recalled. "But there was no way I was getting up and letting them have another play. Taylor cursed at me and told me to get off of him and I did, just as the second hand hit zero. It was a great win and a great achievement because we did not have a lot of talent. I don't know how we did it, but we won the game."

Bednarik was not always on the delivering end when it came to pain. During his 14-year career he missed only three games, two of which were as rookie, but the force of his hitting eventually took its toll on his body. In particular, his hands now look like

THE BEDNARIK FILE

Chuck Bednarik is, at the very least, the greatest Eagle ever. He will always be remembered as the heroic leader of the last Philadelphia football team to win an NFL Championship. Here are a few facts about one of the toughest players to ever put on a helmet.

- Bednarik was born in the heart of America's gridiron breadbasket, in Bethlehem, Pennsylvania, in 1925.
- He was a two-time All America selection at Penn back when the school, now a member of the 1AA Ivy League, was a national power.
- As a junior in 1947, he helped lead Penn to its only undefeated season in a 78-year stretch from 1908 to 1986.
- In 1948 Bednarik became the first offensive lineman to win the Maxwell Award, which is given to the nation's best college football player.
- He finished third in the 1948 Heisman Trophy race and is one of only five offensive linemen in the entire history of the award to finish in the top three. Among the others are Pro Football Hall of Famers Bob Bell of Minnesota and Dick Butkus of Illinois (both played offense and defense in college and became defensive players in the NFL).
- Bednarik was the first pick in the NFL's 1949 draft.
- He was an All-Pro center in 1950 and then became an All-Pro linebacker from 1951 to 1956.
- He played in eight Pro Bowls and was MVP of the 1954 game.
- Bednarik missed only three games during his 14-season career.
- As the NFL's last two-way player in the 12-game 1960 season, Bednarik was on the field for some 600 of a possible 720 minutes. In the 1960 NFL title game, he played more than 58 minutes in a 17–13 victory over Green Bay.
- Bednarik earned a $250 bonus for his two-way effort in 1960.
- He was inducted into the Pro Football Hall of Fame in 1967, after the minimum five-year waiting period had expired.
- In 1969 he was inducted into the College Football Hall of Fame; that year he was also named center on the NFL's all-time team for its first half century.

- The College Defensive Player of the Year Award is named in honor of Chuck Bednarik. Dan Connor of Penn State won the award in 2007.
- Oh yeah, one other thing about Bednarik: in the carefree days of his youth, before going to college and becoming arguably the best player in the history of professional football, Bednarik helped defeat the genocidal tyranny of Nazi Germany during World War II. He spent more than two years in the service and flew 30 missions over Europe as a waist gunner on a B-24 bomber. Needless to say, playing 58 minutes of football and thumping Lombardi's Packers must have been a cozy walk in the park by comparison. They don't make 'em like Bednarik anymore.

something out of a movie—he is unable to extend any of his fingers straight out. They are all bent, gnarled, and misshapen.

Once during a preseason game toward the end of his career, as Bednarik played off a block and made a hit on a runner, he felt a searing pain in his arm. He had torn one of his bicep muscles, which then slipped from his upper arm down to his forearm.

"Chuck pushed the muscle back in its place and went to the sideline," Brookshier said. "He told the doctor to put some tape around it and he went back in. It was an *exhibition* game, and he was playing like it was for the championship. That's the way he played all the time and that's why he became the great player he was." Bednarik recognizes that today's athletes are bigger and stronger than players were during his career. But this 6'3", 235-pound linebacker believes he would still have the same impact on the game today, despite those differences. "A reporter once asked me if I thought I could play with the guys playing today," Bednarik said. "I told him his question was a f---ing insult. Of course I could play today. And I would be a star."

Do you want to argue?

STEVE VAN BUREN

The list of the greatest running backs in league history often includes names like Jim Brown, Marion Motley, Bronko Nagurski, Walter Payton, Gale Sayers, and O.J. Simpson. They were all

Chuck Bednarik may have been the toughest, nastiest player who ever donned an NFL uniform.

named to the All-NFL team that the league put together in 1994 on the occasion of its 75th anniversary. Steve Van Buren was also a part of that group.

Van Buren ran the ball for the Eagles from 1944 through 1951. He was a running back who was much bigger and more powerful than many in his era. Although he could run past defenders, he much preferred to run *over* them. Van Buren never measured his deeds in rushing titles or personal glory. He was old school before that term ever existed. He was happy with his performance if the Eagles won, and he was miserable if they lost.

"That is why I played the game," Van Buren said. "To get the thrill that comes from winning. Individual honors and trophies and titles never meant much to me. I guess I was a little shy. But I sure liked to win."

And win the Eagles did in his era. They won three straight Eastern Conference titles and two NFL titles in 1948 and '49. Van Buren was named to the All-NFL team five times in a six-year period, and he was the main reason his team won.

Former Eagles All-Pro guard Frank "Bucko" Kilroy said that Van Buren was capable of setting his mind to anything and then accomplishing it on the football field. "He was the man and there was no doubt about that," Kilroy said. "He was the best player on our team and he was truly our meal ticket. Not only that, but he became the prototype NFL running back."

At 6'1" and 210 pounds, Van Buren would be a good-sized back in the NFL today. Back in the 1940s, he was like a man among boys. Opponents dripped with fear when he had the ball in full flight. His speed and power were the main ingredients for some horrific collisions that almost always left defenders on the ground writhing in a fair amount of pain. He came to be called "Wham-Bam" because of the sound associated with his impacts.

Van Buren was born in the town of La Ceiba, in the Spanish Honduras, in 1920. He had a difficult childhood that became even tougher when he lost his parents at an early age. He was raised by his grandmother in New Orleans, where his proficiency on the football field led to a scholarship at Louisiana State University.

Until his senior year, Van Buren was more of a blocking back than anything else. He excelled at opening holes for a Tiger running back by the name of Alvin Dark, who went on to play second base for baseball's New York Giants and eventually became a major league manager. During Van Buren's senior year, Head Coach Bernie Moore finally gave him a chance to carry the ball.

The coach was amazed by what he saw and actually apologized to Van Buren for not getting him into the lineup sooner.

The Eagles made Van Buren their first-round draft choice in 1944; he told Eagles general manager Harry Thayer that he wanted $10,000 to sign a contract. Thayer laughed at the idea of paying a rookie that much. When Van Buren then came down with a poorly timed case of appendicitis, Thayer used the opportunity to sign him to a $4,000 contract.

Training camp was scheduled to begin in 10 days, and Van Buren was tightly wrapped as practice started. He took part in practice despite a seven-inch incision where his appendix had been removed. Instead of lauding Van Buren for his courage, Eagles coach Greasy Neale lambasted him for being out of shape as blood oozed out of his wound. It was only at that moment that Van Buren realized how tough life in professional football was going to be.

After piling up yards and team records, Van Buren finally got the championship he wanted in 1948 when the Eagles beat the Chicago Cardinals 7–0 in the snow at Shibe Park. Van Buren scored the game's only touchdown on a five-yard run in snowy conditions. He almost missed the game entirely—the blizzard that was raging before the start of the game was quite blinding, and Van Buren assumed the game would be cancelled. On a whim he ventured to the stadium and was shocked to see fans in the stands. He quickly got dressed and made his contribution.

The following year, Van Buren and the Eagles took on the Los Angeles Rams for the title. It turned out to be a record-setting day in the rain for Van Buren. He ran 31 times for 196 yards, leading the Eagles to a 14–0 title game win.

Hollywood types stopped in the locker room to congratulate Van Buren after the game. One was leading man Clark Gable. The star of *Gone with the Wind* told Van Buren that he was the greatest athlete Gable had ever seen. Van Buren never paid much attention to happenings off the football field—and he didn't know Clark Gable from Clark Kent—but he told his teammates that the mustachioed actor seemed like a nice guy.

Injuries took their toll on Van Buren in 1950 and '51, but he played until he couldn't go on any longer. Torn knee ligaments suffered in practice before the season finally ended his career. When he retired he was the NFL's all-time leading rusher with 5,860 yards and held the league record for touchdowns in a season. For his career he averaged one touchdown for every 19.1 times he touched the ball.

Even though his halcyon days were in the 1940s, Van Buren is still widely remembered in Philadelphia. It speaks to his talent, tenacity, and fortitude that he is still mentioned—and deservedly so—alongside the game's greats.

BOB "BOOMER" BROWN

Let's get it straight. Offensive linemen are always underrated. While coaches and scouts may recognize the talent they have doing all the grunt work from July to January (or February, for Super Bowl teams), the accolades that are piled on players at skill positions rarely come an offensive lineman's way.

Offensive linemen are rarely recognized off the field. Those who are merely good at their position will never be mobbed at the supermarket or their local sports bar. Players who rank with the all-time greats of the game may end up with a bust in the Hall of Fame, but they still just don't get the recognition they truly deserve.

For example, former Bengals offensive tackle Anthony Munoz is recognized as one of the greatest blockers the game has known over the last 25 years. Retired Patriot guard John Hannah has been labeled the best offensive lineman ever by many experts and former opponents, including ex-Eagles defensive lineman "Bucko" Kilroy. But while die-hard fans will certainly recognize a picture of Munoz when they see him, less than half of today's fans would know who "Hawg" Hannah is, let alone recognize his photo.

Bob "Boomer" Brown belongs in the same category as Munoz and Hannah. He was a Hall of Fame tackle who began his superb NFL career with a five-year stint in Philadelphia. He also played for the Los Angeles Rams and the Oakland Raiders, delivering stellar performances for both franchises.

Brown may very well have been the best offensive lineman to

ever play the game. He was not big on talking—and throughout the 1960s and '70s, offensive linemen were not sought out for interviews often, anyway—but he was big, strong, athletic, and mean. Instead of absorbing blows from pass-rushing defensive ends, Brown dished them out, punishing his opponents. His powerful forearm shots would often render opponents useless for long stretches.

Brown has admitted that he enjoyed inflicting pain on the playing field. "When I hit someone right, I knew he would remember who hit him and what it felt like," Brown said. "That was just a part of my game. I was not going to just sit there and let somebody hit me."

Opponents knew Brown was a stellar player with all the stats and technical skills to prove it. He was so dominant that he made even Hall of Famers quake. "When I played against Bob Brown, if I just came out of there alive, I would feel so good," said former Vikings defensive end Carl Eller. Eller joined Brown as a member of pro football's Hall of Fame class of 2004.

Brown was named all-NFL seven times in 10 seasons. The one thing all of his contemporaries agree on is that he was the first offensive lineman to play with a defensive lineman's mentality.

John Madden was Brown's coach with the Raiders before becoming a broadcasting legend. "He was such a dominating player," said Madden. "He was the most aggressive offensive lineman that I think I've ever seen, the most aggressive offensive lineman that ever played."

A first-round Eagles pick out of Nebraska in 1964, Brown was one of the first professional football players to embrace weight training and year-round conditioning. His prowess in the weight room became legendary. "I took to it like a duck to water," Brown said of the weight training. "I went five hours a day, seven days a week." Teammates and opponents didn't necessarily embrace weight training the way Brown did, but when they saw how effective he was on the field, they had to try to keep up with him. Brown became a weight training trendsetter. With his nasty attitude on the field, opponents had no chance if they couldn't match his strength.

Brown earned most of his notoriety while playing for the

Rams and the Raiders—both of whom were playoff teams nearly every year during the last five years of his career. But he probably played his best football with the Eagles. He was at his peak physically, and he had learned the nuances of the game from two of its best teachers: legendary Cornhusker head coach Bob Devaney, who was known as a great instructor, and Eagles offensive line coach Dick Stanfel, who had a similar reputation. Brown learned his lessons thoroughly. Unfortunately, he was the best player on a below average team, and he didn't receive much recognition.

The 6'4", 295-pound Brown was one of the few players on the team who supported embattled head coach Joe Kuharich. Brown said Kuharich was "like a father" to him, and called him a good human being. But he was nearly alone in that opinion; Kuharich was fired in 1969.

Brown felt tremendous responsibility to do his best on every single play no matter what the ramification might be. "It didn't matter a bit to me if we were 11–0 or 0–11," Brown explained. "I was getting paid to do a job, and I was going to give it everything I had. It wasn't enough just to get the better of the guy across from me. I had to give my best and dominate. That's what I was getting paid to do."

The best battles ever produced by the NFL may have been at the Rams practices when Hall of Fame defensive end Deacon Jones battled Brown on an everyday basis. Brown even mentioned Jones when he was inducted into the Hall of Fame. "What really made the Rams experience so good was that every day I had the opportunity to work with and against the greatest defensive end ever, Deacon Jones," said Brown. "Each day, I knew I had to bring my A-game to practice. And I also knew that working against Deacon would surely help me develop my abilities to become a better offensive tackle—my thinking being, if it doesn't kill me, the process will certainly make me stronger. I want to say a special thank you to Deacon, because what he did helped lead me to this."

Jones, whose outsized ego rarely allowed him to recognize anyone else, gave kudos to Brown for his consistency and desire to win. "He was a battler who did the job thoroughly and completely," Jones said. "He didn't want to win; he wanted to dominate. He would bring an ax to kill a mosquito."

Brown had excellent upper body strength to go with his long arms and legs. Those natural assets made him a great pass blocker. But it was his aggressive attitude that took over on running plays; when he exploded off the line on a drive block, the sound of the impact on his target could be heard across the field and in the stands.

One of Dick Vermeil's earliest coaching jobs was as an assistant coach with the Rams in 1969. He got to watch Brown almost daily and was thoroughly impressed with his ability to knock opponents back off the line of scrimmage. "He was clearly one of a kind," Vermeil said. "You just don't see that kind of production on a consistent basis."

Brown moved on to the Raiders in 1971 and played there for the last three years of his career. He played with center Jim Otto, guard Gene Upshaw, and tackle Art Shell, all Hall of Famers. Nevertheless, it was Brown who set the tone for what may have been the best offensive line of all time.

"I learned a whole lot from him," said Shell. "A lot of little things, like how to formulate a plan to attack a defensive end—going into a game trying to have at least three ways to take this guy on. And he was as quick as anybody I've ever seen. He could come out of his stance on a pass set, leap off the ground like a frog, backward, as quick as a hiccup, and then he would lash out at the defensive end. He was unbelievable."

Brown played his last down of professional football in 1973, but it took 31 years for him to be voted into the Hall of Fame. In 2004 he was finally given the spot that he had rightfully earned long before.

THE POLISH RIFLE

Many football fans know Ron Jaworski as a knowledgeable, technically skilled analyst of the game who excels at explaining a quarterback's perspective. "Jaws," as he is often called, understands the offensive game as well as any coach and has been explaining it to fans on ESPN since 1990. In fact, he's done so well

Getty Images

Many fans know Ron Jaworski as the talkative, incisive analyst on *Monday Night Football* **but before that he was a gunslinging quarterback who led the Eagles to a Super Bowl XV appearance against the Raiders.**

that the network promoted him to color analyst on *Monday Night Football* telecasts prior to the 2007 season.

Jaworski comes by his skill as an analyst thanks to tremendous preparation. He is not averse to telling viewers and listeners how much study he undertakes to prepare for each broadcast. It is as if he is campaigning to keep his job every time he goes on the air—which is quite charming, because it shows that even superstars can still harbor a little bit of insecurity about themselves.

Jaworski's appointment as the Monday night analyst is the most impressive move of his post-playing career, but he was also something to behold as a player. He was the thinking man's quarterback, coming into the league in 1973 as a second-round draft choice of the Los Angeles Rams out of tiny Youngstown State University in Ohio.

Jaworski never really had a chance to show off his strong arm in Los Angeles; he threw only 124 passes in three seasons under head coach Chuck Knox. But Jaws used that time on the bench to learn the pro game, watching James Harris and Pat Haden throw the ball for the Rams. Still, though Jaworski enjoyed his time in Los Angeles, the Polish Rifle wanted to play.

While Jaworski was growing restless in Los Angeles, Eagles head coach Dick Vermeil was unhappy with what he was seeing from his own team's nondescript quarterbacks. Roman Gabriel, a former star with the Rams, was past his prime, and backup Mike Boryla just didn't have the consistency of a top quarterback. Vermeil knew that Jaworski had a strong arm and that he had not been used very much by Knox; the two developed an immediate partnership when the Eagles sent tight end Charle Young to the Rams in exchange for the quarterback.

Vermeil didn't necessarily sense a lack of confidence in his new quarterback, but he was determined to make sure Jaworski knew that he was *the* man in Philadelphia. The earnest Vermeil told Jaworski he was going to be the Eagles' quarterback—no matter what. A bad game or two would not send him to the sideline. "Good days or bad, you are my quarterback," Vermeil said. "It may cost us in the beginning, but you're going to start and play no matter what." Vermeil made it a point to reemphasize that in the middle of games, when anger and disappointment often pushes coaches to point fingers and blame certain players. There was none of that between Vermeil and Jaws.

Vermeil's belief in Jaworski enabled the quarterback to make it through his difficult early seasons in Philadelphia. Eagles fans, never shy about showing their displeasure, took a special joy in booing Jaworski. Vermeil let the press know beyond a shadow of a doubt that he believed Jaworski had the talent and the mental makeup needed to be a winning quarterback, and that he was not about to let the fans decide who his quarterback would be.

As a result, Jaworski had plenty of time to develop his game. His ability to throw the ball downfield became an immediate asset to the team. He would regularly throw the ball deep early in the game in an attempt to show defensive backs what they were going to have to defend against. As his experience level grew, he also learned to take advantage of open spots in the zone by throwing underneath to receivers.

Vermeil worked hard to mold Jaworski into a professional quarterback and not just a strong-armed thrower with a catchy nickname. Jaws learned about pace, timing, and exactly how much to take off on his shorter passes. "I owe him quite a bit," Jaworski said. "Yes, I had a strong arm when I came into the league, but I needed to learn about the position and about how to play consistently. He taught me how to be patient and how to play smart football."

By the time the 1979 season started, Jaworski was a winning quarterback. He no longer tried to drill the ball to his receivers on short- and medium-range passes. He could zip it if a receiver was tightly covered and there was just a small window, but he also knew how to take something off the ball and allow his receivers to catch it in stride, without bracing.

In 1979 Jaworski completed 190 of 374 passes for 2,669 yards with 18 touchdowns and 12 interceptions. The Eagles went 11–5 that year and then took out the Bears in the playoffs, 27–17, in their first postseason game since the 1960 championship. They were favored to beat the surprisingly successful Tampa Bay Bucs on the road the following week in the divisional playoffs, but the four-year-old Tampa Bay team came away with a 24–17 win.

The loss was painful and somewhat humiliating for Jaworski and his teammates. It inspired a clear determination not to repeat the previous year's mistakes when training camp began in 1980. The Eagles played like a dominant team, going 12–4 and winning the NFC Championship. Jaworski threw for 3,529 yards and had a career-best 27 touchdown passes.

The Eagles had relatively one-sided victories over the Vikings and the Cowboys in order to earn a spot in the Super Bowl, where they were favored slightly over the Raiders. Philadelphia had beaten Oakland during the regular season, and Jaworski was very confident going in. However, the experienced Raiders were the

Getty Images

Hard-charging running back Wilbert Montgomery is one of the most underrated performers in NFL history.

better team on the field; the Eagles lost a lopsided 27–10 game.

Jaworski, however, was not one to stay down after a loss; he came back in 1981, throwing for 3,095 yards and 23 touchdowns. The team had a 10–6 record and earned a spot in the postseason, but then lost the wild-card playoff game against up-and-coming New York Giants at home. The New York squad featured a nasty rookie linebacker in Lawrence Taylor, perhaps the most punishing player in the league since Chicago's Dick Butkus had created mayhem in the 1960s and '70s. Taylor would prove to be at the top of his game against divisional opponents; with two games a year against the Eagles, he had his sights set on Jaworski.

Jaws knew he was up against it, but he didn't let Taylor's intimidating style get the best of him. Taylor may have punished him relentlessly, but Jaworski never gave in to the fear or the pain. He bounced up to go after the Giants again and again, even if he did keep a wary eye out for Taylor.

Teammates like Mike Quick, Stan Walters, and Wilbert Montgomery all respected Jaws for his heart and enthusiasm, while the coaching staff loved his ability to think through the game and execute. Jaworski would play for the Green and White through the 1986 season before ending his career with one-year stints in Miami and Kansas City. He never got back to the Super Bowl, but his passion for and dedication to the game have shone brightly in his second career as a broadcaster.

A WEST TEXAS HERO

Wilbert Montgomery's heart will always endear him to Eagles fans. So will his legs.

Montgomery was basically an unknown when the Eagles drafted him in the sixth round of the 1977 draft out of tiny Abilene Christian University in west Texas. There was nothing spectacular about Montgomery when Vermeil drafted him. He was on the small side (5'10" and 195 pounds), and while he had good speed, he was not a burner. He did score a record 76 touchdowns despite missing 11 games because of various injuries.

But Vermeil saw a willingness to fight in Montgomery—the ability to put his foot on his opponent's throat—and he knew this was a young man worth bringing into camp. He had the natural instincts to become a great cutback runner, to find the openings needed to make big plays out of nothing.

Montgomery was shocked by the rough-and-tumble world of the NFL. He had attended a very religious college where there were few raised voices and no coarse language. Nearly every other word he heard in his first training camp was profane. Still, none of it stopped him from making an impression on the field. He started out as an outstanding kick returner, leading the NFC with an average of 26.9 yards per return. The more Vermeil looked at Montgomery, the more he liked him. Vermeil made Montgomery the starter in 1978, and his insertion into the lineup paid immediate dividends. He ran for 1,220 yards and nine touchdowns and also showed fine receiving skills, catching 34 passes. By his second year he was a dynamic part of the Eagles offense, and he was hungry for more.

While the Eagles staff was concerned that Montgomery seemed to initiate as much contact as he absorbed, they were not about to change his style. He had breakaway ability on the field even if he was not the fastest guy by the stopwatch; more importantly, he also showed a talent to play physical football and to win against bigger players.

Nobody was happier about Montgomery's running ability and consistency than Jaworski, who needed the team to have a solid running game to take some of the pressure off. Finally, Jaworski did not have to do everything by himself—Montgomery was often able to hit the home run after Jaws had gone downfield a few times. When the Eagles sensed that their opponent was looking to stop a medium-range or deep pass, Montgomery would regularly get the call on the draft or counter play. It turned out to be a great game plan for the Eagles.

"What a great running back Wilbert Montgomery was for us," said Jaworski. "It wasn't that he was the fastest or strongest player at his position, but he did everything well and he did it at big moments. He was so talented and so dependable. His instincts to make the right move at the right time made him a standout player.

Montgomery improved on his rushing total in 1979, picking up 1,512 yards on 338 bone-rattling carries. He rushed for nine touchdowns and also caught 41 passes for 494 yards and five touchdowns. The Eagles tied for first with Dallas in the NFC East that year; the Cowboys were awarded the division title because they had a better conference record. The Eagles still made the playoffs, defeating the Chicago Bears 27–17 in the wild-card round. But when they went to Tampa Bay for their divisional playoff game against the Bucs, the defense could not stop the

THE TROPHY

Harold Carmichael was undoubtedly one of the greatest receivers in Eagles history.

"High" Harold—he was 6'10" in his football spikes—became a record-setting player during the 1979 season. When he caught a 5-yard pass from Ron Jaworski in Week 10 of the 1979 season against the Cleveland Browns, it marked the 106th straight game that Carmichael had caught at least one pass.

Carmichael had no idea he was close to breaking a record held by Danny Abramowicz of the Saints until a local television producer in Philadelphia counted up the games and told Carmichael about his achievement.

While Carmichael was intrigued by his chance to make history prior to that game, Eagles owner Leonard Tose was not about to let the achievement go unnoticed. He had a huge trophy made to celebrate the achievement.

Carmichael—the tallest receiver in the league—was given the tallest trophy ever made to celebrate his achievement. Tose had a trophy built that was 23 feet tall and handed it to him in the middle of the game. The Guinness Book of World Records said the trophy was 8 feet taller than the previous record holder.

The trophy was too big for Carmichael's house or even the Eagles' corporate offices. Instead, it was transported to the Pro Football Hall of Fame in Canton, where it sat in the lobby for several years.

Carmichael held the record until 1986 when it was subsequently broken by Seattle wide receiver Steve Largent.

running of Ricky Bell, while the Tampa Bay defense focused on stopping Montgomery.

Tampa Bay Hall of Fame defensive end Lee Roy Selmon knew his work was cut out for him in that game: in addition to getting after Montgomery, he also had to battle Eagles All-Pro tackle Stan Walters. With Bell giving his defensive teammates plenty of time to rest, the Bucs were basically fresh the entire game and were able to beat Philadelphia 24–17.

"Stopping Montgomery was priority number one for us," said Selmon. "We thought everything they did was keyed off of getting Wilbert going. You could tell that their confidence level would get very high when Montgomery started to cook, so we were just not going to let that happen. We got a big assist from our offense, because they put points on the board and kept Montgomery off the field."

Injuries forced Montgomery to miss four games during the 1980 regular season and held his rushing total to just 778 yards, but he was not about to be just a spectator during the postseason. The Eagles won the NFC East with a 12–4 record; after defeating Minnesota 31–16 in the divisional playoffs, they had an opportunity to earn their first spot in the Super Bowl if they could beat the archrival Cowboys at home. Throughout the week prior to the game, there were serious doubts about Montgomery's ability to suit up and play effectively, but he was not going to allow himself to miss this opportunity.

Montgomery set the tone for the game when he scored on a 42-yard run early in the first quarter. He started left but then cut back to his right, taking advantage of beautiful blocks by right guard Woody Peoples (on Cowboy defensive tackle Larry Cole) and right tackle Stan Walters (on huge defensive end Ed "Too Tall" Jones). Montgomery zipped through the hole and accelerated until he reached the end zone. He ran for 194 yards that day, becoming the first back to run for more than 100 yards against the Cowboys in the postseason. The Eagles won, 20–7, earning the right to play against the Raiders in Super Bowl XV.

Dallas head coach Tom Landry was duly impressed with Montgomery's performance. "I've known for quite some time what Wilbert Montgomery is capable of if you let him run loose, and that's just what we did," Landry said. "Take nothing away from him, because he is a great back who played well. We had a chance to grab the momentum several times. We didn't, and they took advantage of their chances."

The Eagles were favored by three and a half points to beat the Raiders in the Super Bowl. Philadelphia had beaten the Raiders during the regular season, and the oddsmakers believed they would be able to repeat their performance. However, Raiders owner Al Davis and head coach Tom Flores were not about to let Montgomery punish them the way he had the Cowboys. Stopping Montgomery was the focus of their defensive game plan, and it worked: the Raiders were able to hold him to just 44 yards on 16 carries. Once the Eagles realized it was not going to be Montgomery's day, Jaworski was forced to carry the burden by himself—and he was unable to do it. The Raiders came away with a 27–10 upset.

Montgomery would bounce back with an explosive 1,402-yard season in 1981 that saw him average a career-best 4.9 yards per carry. However, his physical style of play was finally starting to catch up with him; he would not top 789 yards in any of the four seasons that followed. Three of those seasons were with the Eagles, but he was traded to the Lions for linebacker Garry Cobb prior to the 1985 season. He played seven games in Detroit before deciding to retire.

Montgomery finished his career as the team's all-time leader in rushing yards (6,538) and attempts (1,465). His name replaced Steve Van Buren in the Eagles record books, and he will always be remembered for his Walter Payton–like all-around play and his long touchdown run against the Cowboys that sent the Birds to their first Super Bowl.

MOMENTS TO SAVOR

THE IMPROBABLE 1960 CHAMPIONS

Remember the great Green Bay teams led by Vince Lombardi in the 1960s? How could anyone forget them? They dominated a Baltimore Colts team that had Hall of Fame talent up and down the roster. They whipped the Dallas Cowboys in two NFL Championship games that were destined to go down as classics. And they upheld the honor of the NFL when they beat the Kansas City Chiefs and the Oakland Raiders in the first two Super Bowls.

Yes, Lombardi's team had it all—and they were especially dominant in the postseason. But of all the teams they played when a championship was on the line, they were unable to get the job done when they came to Franklin Field on December 26, 1960, to take on the Eagles.

Head coach Buck Shaw had a team of hustlers and clever players, but outside of Hall of Famer Chuck Bednarik and an aging Norm Van Brocklin, this team did not have a very high talent level. In fact Bednarik was amazed that they were able to beat out the Giants and the Browns for the Eastern Conference title—let alone take on the mighty Packers and win. But on a day that was bathed in sunshine, Lombardi's team just didn't have the consistency that would become their hallmark in the coming decade.

The most memorable play of this game was the last snap. Jim Taylor caught a dump-off pass from Bart Starr and was busting to get to the goal line, but was brought down by a combination of Bednarik and Bobby Jackson. The final seconds then ticked away to give the Eagles a 17–13 win while Bednarik held Taylor down.

Although the Eagles played sensational defensive football throughout the game, the contest did not start out in a memorable fashion. Running back Timmy Brown, a former Packer and a future Hollywood actor, took Paul Hornung's kickoff and returned it 20 yards to the Eagles' 22. On the first play from scrimmage, a Van Brocklin pass into the flat was intercepted by Packers defensive lineman Bill Quinlan at the 14-yard line.

Lombardi wanted to intimidate the Eagles by using the Packers' power running game, featuring Taylor and Hornung. After three plays the Packers had reached the Eagles' 7-yard line and were faced with a fourth-down decision. Lombardi believed his team had superior manpower up front and great talent in the backfield; showing little respect for an Eagles team that he believed had only ordinary talent, he decided to go for it. Taylor got the ball one more time. But linebacker Maxie Baughan overpowered Packer receiver Max McGee, who was blocking on the play. Baughan brought down Taylor after a gain of just a yard and the Eagles offense took over.

Stopping the Packers had given the Eagles plenty of momentum and confidence. On a third-and-five play from the Eagles' 10, running back Ted Dean slashed for 10 yards before he fumbled; Bill Forester recovered for Green Bay. Once again, the Eagles defense played without any give. The Packers got a first down, but that was it. Starr threw a couple of incomplete passes and then Hornung kicked a field goal to give Green Bay a 3–0 lead.

Van Brocklin fumbled the next snap after the kickoff but was able to recover. The Eagles got one first down before having to punt back to Green Bay. The Packers were able to move the ball into Eagles territory, but the Eagles pass defense forced Starr into three consecutive incomplete attempts. Green Bay had to settle for another Hornung field goal, taking a 6–0 lead early in the second quarter.

After an exchange of punts, the Eagles finally got the ball in decent field position when they took over in Green Bay territory. Van Brocklin, a future Hall of Famer who was not about to get nervous over his poor start, found wide receiver Tommy

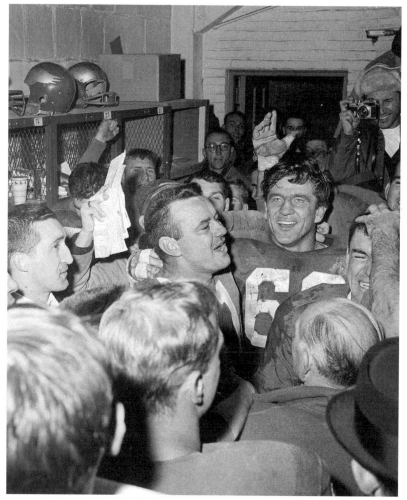

Norm Van Brocklin, left, who quarterbacked the Eagles to a 17–13 win over the Green Bay Packers on December 27, 1960, in the NFL championship game in Philadelphia, celebrates with teammates in the dressing room at Franklin Field. With him is Chuck Bednarik. Van Brocklin said he planned to retire after the title game.

McDonald with a 22-yard pass and then a 35-yard touchdown strike that left the Packers shaken.

Green Bay was unable to do anything on its next possession, giving Van Brocklin a shot of confidence when the Eagles got the ball back. Starting at the Philadelphia 26, he marched the team downfield to the Packer 8, where the drive stalled. Bobby Walston kicked a field goal to push the Eagles' lead to 10–6. The Packers had one more chance before the end of the first half, driving quickly from their own 20 to the Eagles' 7. But Hornung then inexplicably missed a 13-yard field-goal attempt on the last play of the half.

Green Bay had dominated the game statistically, but the Eagles had the halftime lead. Although the Packers domination on paper continued in the third quarter, the scoreboard did not move. The frustration was palpable on the Green Bay sideline. That would change in the fourth quarter.

Hornung had been forced to the sideline after getting smashed by a Bednarik tackle, so backup Tom Moore had come in to alternate carries with Taylor. The running game worked successfully and the Packers were at the Eagles' 7 when Starr found McGee with a touchdown pass. The touchdown sent a surge of despair through the crowd, who could sense the favored Packers taking over the game. Their fears, however, were not to be realized; Dean took the ensuing kickoff at his own 3-yard line and returned it 58 yards to the Green Bay 39.

Despite the change in momentum, Dean was mad at himself. His teammates had provided perfect blocking on the play, and he thought he should have been able to take the ball to the end zone. "They set it up perfectly for me," Dean said. "I was supposed to fake to my right and then hit the lane up the sideline. With the blocking I had, I should have made it."

Still, the Eagles were not about to waste this opportunity. They pounded away at the Packer defense with their ground game, using Dean and Billy Ray Barnes to do most of the damage. After Green Bay sacked Van Brocklin, the Dutchman hit Barnes with a 13-yard pass. In the resulting third-and-one play, Barnes punished the Packers with a five-yard run.

Throughout both the drive and the game, the Eagles were attempting almost all of their runs to their right. But on a first-and-goal play, Dean swept four yards over the left side. He followed that with another play over the left side, a five-yard touchdown.

Dean followed the blocking of offensive lineman Gerry Huth on the play that turned out to be the game-winning touchdown. Ironically, Huth, who had been with the Giants prior to coming to the Eagles, had learned the intricacies of blocking on the power sweep from Lombardi himself when Vince was an assistant coach in New York.

Huth was jubilant after the game. "I wanted to go to the Green Bay locker room and thank Vince Lombardi," Huth said. "When Lombardi and I were both in New York, he made me practice that sweep hundreds of times. I wanted to tell him, 'I ran it just the way you taught me,' but I didn't think he'd be in the mood to hear it."

Dean's fourth-quarter touchdown gave the Eagles a 17–13 lead. But the Packers still had opportunities to come back and win the title. On their final drive, Starr hit Taylor and Moore with first-down producing plays. But as the clock wound down, the Packers had the ball at the Eagles' 22 with no timeouts and only 12 seconds left. Starr flipped the ball to Taylor, who put his head down and started charging like a bull.

Against any other linebacker, Taylor might have been able to win the battle by putting his shoulder to his tackler's midsection. But that strategy would not work against Bednarik, who met the tank-like Taylor with his own brute force. The result was a brutal tackle at the 9. Bednarik lay on top of Taylor as the clock went down to 0:00 and the gun went off. Taylor had been fighting Bednarik, attempting to push him off so the Packers could get one more play in. "After the gun I got up and told Taylor he could get up now," Bednarik recalled. "'The f*cking game is over.'"

Everyone was exhausted after the game—with the possible exception of Bednarik. He had played 139 of the 142 plays from scrimmage, serving on both the offense and the defense. His performance was made all the more remarkable by the fact that he was 35 years old. "I didn't get tired," Bednarik said. "Once the game started, my adrenaline was pumping. The weather was nice. It was 40 degrees, which is just cold enough but not too cold. It's all mind over matter anyway. When you are on the field in the fourth quarter of a championship game, you don't get tired. You do everything you are capable of...and then a little more."

It was perhaps the greatest moment in the history of sports in Philadelphia. The Sixers have had two NBA championships since, while the Phillies won their only World Series 20 years later. The Flyers won back-to-back Stanley Cups in 1974 and '75, with a sensational team. But Philadelphia fans who can remember the 1960 NFL Championship believe that was the sweetest win of them all.

And no one with the Packers will ever come close to forgetting it.

THE 1980 NFC CHAMPIONSHIP: BIRDS TAKE WING

The Philadelphia Eagles knew they had arrived. Now they just had to prove it to the rest of the NFL. After an outstanding regular season and a convincing 31–16 win over the Vikings in the first round of the playoffs, they were on the precipice of glory. If they could win one game against the Dallas Cowboys, they would earn their first trip to the Super Bowl.

The Eagles had forced the Cowboys into the wild-card role after winning the NFC East under head coach Dick Vermeil. Dallas appeared to be sleepwalking in their divisional playoff game against the Falcons. They were trailing 24–10 in the fourth quarter, but despite their lackluster performance they came back to take a surprising 30–27 victory.

Prior to the game, the team practiced in Tampa. Even though the game was to be played at the Vet, Vermeil wanted his team to get its work done under ideal weather conditions.

Throughout the week, Eagles players talked to the media about their respect for Dallas, and Ron Jaworski sounded as if he was overwhelmed by the thought of battling their flex defense. They publicly acknowledged that they felt it would be very hard to stay on the field with the great Cowboys team. Vermeil also seemed a bit intimidated at the thought of matching wits with Tom Landry, intimating that he didn't feel as if he belonged on the same field with old Tom. "I was a high school coach in California when he was coaching against Green Bay in the championship game," Vermeil said with an aw-shucks tone. The smell of fear was palpable.

Actually, it was all a set up. Vermeil did a masterful job of preparing his team for the psychological battle with the Cowboys. The Eagles were acting as if the task in front of them may have been too daunting, but in reality they were ready to dominate. They did not feel the least bit intimidated by the Cowboys' reputation. As a matter of fact, they felt quite confident that they would be able to have their way with the Cowboys—they were bigger and stronger and knew how to impose their will on their opponents.

"We used you guys," Jaworski admitted to the media later. "The coach gave us instructions on how to deal with the press. It was a perfect setup. We wanted to inflate the Cowboys' egos. In the meetings we knew we were going to win, but we acted worried. You'll remember that I threw a pass into the blocking sled and acted all concerned when you were standing around."

Still, the Eagles did have their concerns, particularly regarding the health of Wilbert Montgomery. Their do-it-all running back had a slew of bumps and bruises from a season's worth of contact. Of particular concern was a balky knee that forced him out of practice prior to the game. There was no question that he would play, but no one knew if he would be effective or how long he would even be able to stay in.

The Cowboys brought a certain swagger and attitude with them wherever they went. When they walked on the turf at Veterans Stadium, they acted as if they already had the game wrapped up. "The Cowboys shouldn't have read the papers," Eagles linebacker Jerry Robinson told *Sports Illustrated* after the game. "You could tell from the way they walked on the field that they already had their bags packed for New Orleans."

Tom Landry and Tex Schramm were banking on Cowboys "superiority" having at least some impact on the Eagles. But the Eagles struck the first blow in the psychological warfare department, choosing to wear their white uniforms at home. Normally, Vermeil dressed his team in green at home; however, it was well-known that the Cowboys loved playing in their white and silver uniforms and felt uncomfortable playing in blue. Schramm and the Cowboys were angered by Vermeil's gamesmanship, but there was nothing they could do about it.

The questions concerning Montgomery were answered very

early in the game. On the Eagles' second offensive play, he ran 42 yards for a touchdown that lit a fuse in the crowd and gave the Eagles sideline the energy they needed. The play was a perfect combination of timing, execution, and luck. The Eagles had much of their passing personnel in the game and the Cowboys were anticipating that Jaworski would line them up in a shotgun formation. Instead, the Eagles went into a power I formation. Dallas was caught with its nickel personnel on the field and got gashed. The Eagles got outstanding blocking from all five of their offensive linemen. In particular, guard Petey Perot got the best of future Hall of Famer Randy White, while center Guy Morriss obliterated linebacker Bob Breunig. Montgomery went untouched into the end zone.

The Cowboys would tie it up in the second quarter on a three-yard run by Tony Dorsett, but that was the last time the Cowboys got beyond the 39-yard line. The Eagles rolled to a 20–7 win that was not as close as the score would seem to indicate.

The Eagles defensive performance was impressive. They held Danny White, Drew Pearson, and Dorsett to 206 total yards and punished the Cowboys with a physical beating. Think Joe Frazier mashing Jimmy Ellis—*that* kind of beating. Eagles defensive coordinator Marion Campbell had been embarrassed when Dallas beat Philadelphia 35–27 less than a month earlier. Campbell did not change the game plan, but he emphasized his points a little more demonstratively in practice. "We didn't do anything different—we just did it better," Campbell said.

If the Eagles were punishing on defense, they were relentless on offense, using a pile-driving running game. Not only did Montgomery run for 194 yards on a sore knee, but fullback Leroy Harris added 60 yards and a touchdown on 10 carries. Prior to that game, Harris had been known more for his love of donuts than for his ability to reach the end zone.

Neither Jaworski nor Danny White was able to do a great deal of damage in the windy conditions that day. Jaworski, NFC Player of the Year, managed only 91 yards, hitting on nine of 29 attempts with two interceptions. Danny White, in his first title bout, connected on 12 of 31 attempts for 127 yards and gave up one interception. Jaworski, however, was instrumental in directing his team to seven third-down conversions in 15 attempts, a significant achievement combined with the Eagles' ball-control attack. By the end of the game, Eagles fans were celebrating in much the same fashion as they had in October when the Phillies won the World Series. Jaworski especially took great joy in beating America's team.

Vermeil, however, wanted more. He wanted a Super Bowl title, and in order to get it he wanted his team to return to the practice field in full pads the very next day. That strategy may not have helped in Super Bowl XV, which the Eagles lost. But it was clearly Vermeil's signature.

The Cowboy Perspective

When the Cowboys rolled into the Vet with an opportunity to win the NFC Championship against the Eagles, they did it with bravado, attitude, and more than their share of arrogance. The players believed that their vast experience in big-game situations would see them through, even if the game was being played in minus-17 windchill conditions.

But to the Philadelphia Eagles it was all new, and the team that had earned no championship banner for two decades played like a group of men fearful that this chance might not pass their way again.

For 60 bone-rattling minutes the Eagles hammered away at the Cowboys, clearly proving their superiority. They did it by holding back the league's highest scoring offense. They also used the punishing Montgomery as if he was Walter Payton or Jim Brown. Despite playing on a very sore knee, he crushed the Cowboy defense every time he touched the ball. His 194 rushing yards took the life out of the Cowboy defense. There was no miracle finish for Coach Landry's team that day.

Tied at halftime, the game turned in the Eagles favor in the third quarter, when three Dallas turnovers resulted in 10 points that provided Vermeil's inspired squad a 17–7 lead to take into the final 15 minutes. "The third quarter," Landry told the media, "was the whole ballgame. We felt if we could win the third quarter, we would be in pretty good shape, but instead we turned the ball over to them three times in good field position. You give a good team that many opportunities, and it's very hard to beat it."

The first costly exchange took place after Cowboys quarterback Danny White, blindsided by Eagles end Carl Hairston while attempting to pass, lost the ball; end Dennis Harrison recovered at the Dallas 11. That turnover resulted in a 26-yard Tony Franklin field goal midway through the period.

The next error came immediately on the heels of a big play that had game-changing momentum written all over it. Trailing by three points, Dallas had just picked up one of its rare third-down conversions; Danny White next zeroed in on tight end Jay Saldi for a 28-yard gain to the Eagles' 40. On the following play, however, running back Dorsett attempted to find daylight to his left and fumbled; linebacker Robinson fell on the ball, got up, and returned it 22 yards to the Cowboys' 38 before being swarmed. Six plays later Harris scored, and the game was over.

Dorsett, the obvious target of Philadelphia's defense all day (gaining only 41 yards in his 13 carries), called his fumble the day's most critical play. "I feel responsible for losing the game," he said afterward. "That fumble was the big play."

Perhaps, but it wasn't the only reason the Cowboys were eliminated. There was little rhythm to their offense; Danny White was repeatedly rushed on his passing attempts and only fullback Robert Newhouse, using misdirection plays to his advantage early, saw running room. Danny White's punting game, usually a strong suit for Dallas, failed repeatedly to get the Cowboys out of trouble; he averaged only 33.7 yards on seven kicks.

In the first half, Dallas got inside the Eagles' 40-yard line only once, on a second-period scoring drive that enabled them to rest at intermission with a 7–7 tie. "Our execution just wasn't clicking," said wide receiver Butch Johnson. "We didn't get the third-down plays like we're supposed to." Only four times in 14 tries did the Cowboys sustain drives after reaching the critical third-down crossroad, and one of those was rendered pointless by the Dorsett fumble.

Landry was fairly happy with the performance of his defense, but the opportunities given to the Philadelphia offense were just too

Getty Images

Defensive end Reggie White combined superb talent with an outsized personality to help give the Eagles one of the most intimidating defenses in the 1990s.

numerous to keep the dam from bursting. "We turned them back a number of times deep in our own end of the field," he said. "But the turnovers gave them the momentum they needed to keep coming."

The best aspect of the game for the Cowboys was their defensive play in the first half after giving up Montgomery's 42-yard touchdown blast. The Eagles threatened regularly after that, but came away with nothing. Philadelphia advanced to Dallas's 23 before a 41-yard field-goal attempt by Franklin was batted down by Aaron Mitchell. On its next series it moved to the 22, and again Franklin came on. But Jaworski, serving as holder, mishandled the ball, and again the Eagles got naught for their efforts.

In the second quarter, after Dallas had tied the game, Jaworski hit wide receiver Harold Carmichael with a 25-yard touchdown shot—but it was called back because guard Woody Peoples grabbed oncoming defender John Dutton by the face mask.

Dallas's only points came on a 10-play, 68-yard drive that lent early hope to their cause. In a march that saw Newhouse gain much of his 44-yard total for the game, Dallas took almost six minutes to get to the Eagles' 3, where Dorsett powered off right tackle for the touchdown with 5:50 remaining in the half.

"We were still very much in it at that time," Landry said. "They had been playing with great enthusiasm, a lot of emotion. But I felt if we could come out and take charge in the second half, we could win it."

For once, Landry's faith in the Cowboys wasn't vindicated. The day clearly belonged to Philadelphia. The Vet had never enjoyed a happier football day—and it would never reach that level again.

THE MINISTER OF DEFENSE

If there was one player more responsible for leading the Eagles to becoming regular playoff contenders in the 1980s and early '90s, it was Reggie White. The Minister of Defense was a one-man tornado on the field who could overpower opponents, run by them, and use an array of moves to beat them on the pass rush. Against the run, he had the technique of Hall of Famer Merlin Olsen and the energy of Deacon Jones. He was a 6'5", 290-pound wrecking crew who loved the camaraderie of the game as much as the contact.

White, an ordained Baptist minister, had a gentle, gregarious, and loving nature off the field. The game of football was seemingly at odds with his religious calling, but White never bought into that argument. "The good Lord has gifted me with the ability to play football," White once said. "What kind of man would I be if I ignored such a gift?"

Many believe that White was the greatest defensive player of his era. Buddy Ryan, his hard-to-please head coach, took it even further. "Reggie is the most gifted defensive player I have ever been around," Ryan said. "He is almost 300 pounds and runs a 4.6 40 [a 4.6-second 40-yard dash]. If you wanted to make the perfect defensive player, you would take Reggie's ingredients and you would have him." In addition to coaching Hall of Famers Dan Hampton and Mike Singletary in Chicago, Ryan was an assistant coach on Bud Grant's outstanding Minnesota Vikings teams in the 1970s and Weeb Ewbank's 1968 Super Bowl Champion Jets team. He coached Jim Marshall, Carl Eller, Alan Page, and Paul Krause in Minnesota, and was known for his demanding standards.

White came to the Eagles after playing for two seasons in the soon-to-be-defunct United States Football League. His first game with the Eagles came in week four of the 1985 season, and he was unstoppable from the start, recording 2.5 sacks and 10 stops in his first game. He was a monster on the field that season with 13 sacks, winning the NFL Defensive Rookie of the Year award. He was viewed as an impossible assignment by opposing offensive linemen and coaches, who had to double or triple team him in order to have any chance at stopping him.

White was the heart of the Philadelphia defense during his eight-year run with the Eagles, recording double-digit sacks each season. But as overwhelming as his numbers were, his value as a team player meant even more. He was a superstar on the field, but he was also as decent a person as has ever played in the NFL, and he was loved by his teammates.

The Eagles defensive line at that time—White, Jerome Brown, Clyde Simmons, and Mike Golic—was a deadly group, and much of it had to do with the way their personalities meshed. The only thing that they lacked was a media friendly nickname. Because they lack a catchy tag like "The Fearsome Foursome" (of the Rams), "The Purple People Eaters" (of the Vikings), or "The Steel Curtain" (of the Steelers, of course), this front four does not come to mind as one of the best groups of all time. But that's exactly what it was—and any quarterback who played against them will vouch for it.

Giants quarterback Phil Simms played against that group twice a year, and keeping an eye on White was always half the battle for him. "That was a nasty group, and Reggie was just an awesome player," Simms said. "It was hard to sleep well the night before facing Reggie. He could just put on an overwhelming show and dominate."

After the 1992 season, White's career with the Eagles came to an end. He got into a dispute with the team when they hired his agent, Patrick Forte, as a team executive. White was upset with both the team and Forte because of the conflict of interest. How could Forte represent White's best interests at the same time as he was seeking employment with the team? He was also upset that Eagles owner Norman Braman had decided not to re-sign much of the team's veteran talent. The Eagles were losing players as a result of free agency, and White did not want to give his all to an organization that he felt was no longer interested in winning.

White shocked the NFL world by signing with the Green Bay Packers in 1993, and he helped transform the Green Bay defense into a nasty unit. That was all they needed to become an elite team; Green Bay dominated the league in 1996, beating New England 35–21 in Super Bowl XXXI. White made the most of his opportunity on sports' biggest stage, sacking New England quarterback Drew Bledsoe three times.

Throughout his career with Philadelphia, Green Bay, and Carolina, White combined dominance on the field with a humble attitude off of it. He took his work seriously, but the most important things in his life were his commitment to his family and God. When his career concluded following the 2000 season with the Panthers, White laid out a plan to help people and preach his Christian beliefs, which he did with joy and passion.

White always said what was on his mind and no one ever doubted his sincerity. However, during a 1998 speech before the Wisconsin state assembly, White made himself a target for critics with a speech that stereotyped a slew of ethnic and racial groups by pointing to their "talents" and "abilities." The idea was a noble one, but the execution was clumsy and awkward. White and his speech became fodder for David Letterman, Jay Leno, and sports talk show hosts around the nation.

White died tragically of respiratory failure in 2004. The shocking death, just a week after his 43rd birthday, left a cavernous hole in the hearts of football fans throughout the nation. The grief was particularly anguished in Philadelphia and Green Bay, where his contributions and achievements will never be forgotten.

DADDY DEAREST

JOE KUHARICH

The Eagles were in a transition period when they hired Joe Kuharich as their head coach in 1964. The legendary Buck Shaw had retired after Philadelphia won the NFL Championship and his replacement, Nick Skorich, flamed out with a 15–24–3 record over the next three years. There was no way that Eagle fans would abide the low-key Skorich any longer; Kuharich was brought in to turn things around.

Why owner Jerry Wolman thought that Kuharich had the wherewithal to get the Eagles back on track is a great mystery. Kuharich was a one-of-a-kind head coach during his previous job at Notre Dame, but not in a good way—he led the Irish to a 17–23 record from 1959 to 1962, becoming the only coach to ever have a losing record at Notre Dame. But while Kuharich may not have had much going for him, he was one of the most thick-skinned coaches the game has ever known—which was lucky for him, as he was disliked by his players, vilified by the fans, and torn to shreds by the media.

Eagles fans were skeptical about Kuharich from the beginning. He had inherited bad situations before, and he had made them all worse. But that did not matter to Wolman. He gave his coach an unheard-of 15-year contract.

Larry Merchant is best known today as a boxing analyst on HBO. But before he went to television, he earned his way as a reporter and columnist in Philadelphia and New York. Merchant was in Philadelphia during Kuharich's disastrous run from 1964 through 1968, and his reaction to Kuharich was typical of the press that followed the team during those awful times. He described Kuharich's five years in Philadelphia as a "reign of error." He also recalled what happened when Wolman sold the team to Leonard Tose. The ink on the contracts had not even dried before Tose tossed Kuharich out on his ear. At that moment an audible roar could be heard throughout the city. The team had been rescued.

Kuharich was at the bottom of his game with Philadelphia:

• He traded outstanding wide receiver Tommy McDonald to Dallas for punter/place-kicker Sam Baker. The Cowboys also threw in obscure offensive lineman Lynn Hoyem and defensive tackle John Meyers. McDonald was a Hall of Famer who was loved by the fans.

• He traded Sonny Jurgensen, perhaps the best pure passer in the game, to the Redskins for Norm Snead.

• He traded away stud linebackers Maxie Baughan and Lee Roy Caffey. He also sent cornerback Irv Cross packing. He did the same with offensive guard Pete Case.

In addition to those trades, Kuharich was an irascible sort who wore on his players' nerves. Star tight end Pete Retzlaff and offensive lineman Ed Blaine both decided to retire rather than take orders from this blowhard.

If Kuharich had no skill at evaluating personnel, he was even worse when it came to game planning. The biggest issue was his poor communication skills. For example, Jurgensen, still the starting quarterback at the time, once had an hour-long meeting with Kuharich to discuss the team's game plan. When reporters asked Jurgensen what Kuharich had said to him, the quarterback just shook his head. "You've talked to him before," Jurgensen said. "Who knows what he said."

Jurgensen's lack of understanding was perhaps largely due to Kuharich's tendency to talk out of both sides of his mouth. He was evasive, ungrammatical, and just plain wrongheaded.

Among the pearls that came out of his mouth:
- "Trading quarterbacks is rare but not unusual."
- "Every coach must view a player with three different eyes."
- "The charge on that blocked kick came either from the inside or the outside."

There were many more misstatements, but Kuharich probably set the all-time record for dunderheadedness when he was asked to explain what happened in a 1966 loss to the Cowboys. Said Kuharich: "A missed block here, a missed assignment there: it all adds up." Had the Eagles lost to the Cowboys by a field goal or a last-minute touchdown? No. All those individual mistakes somehow added up to a humiliating 56–7 beating.

During the 1968 season, Kuharich's Eagles were at their worst. They were a sad club that suffered through loss after loss. By the time they went to Detroit for a game in late November, they were 0–11. However, the pain of all that losing did leave one potential reward clearly in sight: if the Eagles could go winless or win no more than one game of their final three, they would end up with the first pick in the NFL draft. That year a spectacular running back named Orenthal James Simpson was leaving USC and heading toward the NFL. He was clearly the best player in the draft, possibly even the best player to join the NFL in years. All the Eagles had to do was continue to lose and they would get him.

Wouldn't you know it? Kuharich's team blanked Detroit 12–0 and beat New Orleans 29–17 the following week. Losing the season finale to Minnesota did them no good. It would now be the Buffalo Bills who had the number one choice in the draft, and they of course took Simpson. While he would become even more famous for his off-the-field issues long after his playing career came to an end, Simpson is still widely recognized as one of the greatest backs the game has ever known.

Kuharich actually had one winning season during his run with the Eagles, going 9–5 in 1966. It marked only the second time in his career that he won more games than he lost. Coaches who lose as much as Kuharich did usually don't get the opportunity to do so for 15 years. Losing remained a way of life for the Eagles under Jerry Williams, Ed Khayat, and Mike McCormack, but those men were head and shoulders above Kuharich when it came to leading a team.

Kuharich couldn't evaluate personnel, he couldn't teach, and he utterly failed to motivate his players. He clearly earned the triple crown.

DICK VERMEIL

Former Eagles owner Leonard Tose was a man who was ruined by gambling. But before he lost everything in the wee hours of the morning during his ill-conceived and alcohol-fueled gambling runs in Atlantic City, he had been a successful businessman. In fact, he had done so well in the trucking business that he was able to buy the woeful Eagles franchise in 1969.

The team did not enjoy one winning season during Tose's first seven years as steward, and by the end of the 1975 season, he was a very frustrated man. He had fired Kuharich upon buying the team, a move that made him a local hero—Kuharich was among the most despised men in the history of Philadelphia sports. After firing Kuharich, Tose tried out Williams, Khayat, and McCormack at the helm, but none of those coaches achieved any success for the team, and the owner was at the end of his rope following the 4-10, 1975 season. He fired McCormack based on the team's lack of progress, but had no clue where to turn for the Eagles' next leading man. He had interviewed big names like Hank Stram, Allie Sherman, and Norm Van Brocklin, but none of them had impressed him.

As he sat down in front of his television to watch the New Year's Day bowl games, Tose expected to see Woody Hayes's powerful Ohio State team thrash a quick, flashy UCLA squad that the experts said was neither big enough nor strong enough to compete with the Buckeyes. But on that particular day, UCLA not only traded punches with Ohio State, they came away with a relatively easy 23–10 win.

Tose had never heard of Dick Vermeil, the young UCLA coach who had engineered the win. But he was impressed with Vermeil's

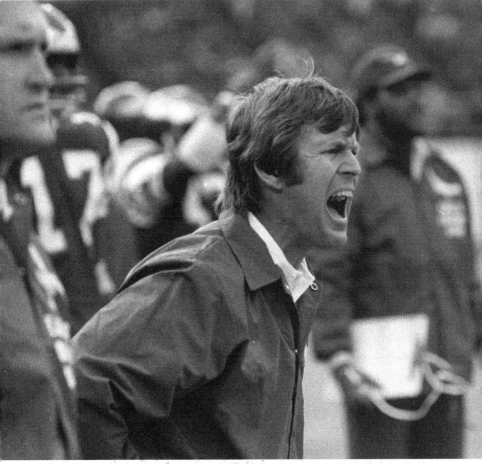

Dick Vermeil's youthful exuberance and nonstop work ethic helped turn the Eagles from bottom feeders to playoff team in just two seasons.

electric personality and the way UCLA played. He instructed Eagles general manager Jim Murray to bring Vermeil in and interview him for the head coaching position.

The idea turned out to be the best thing to happen to the franchise since the 1960 championship season. Vermeil, a 39-year-old coach with great aspirations, was as bright in person as he seemed on the television screen. The Eagles may have been saddled with losing season after losing season, and the Philadelphia area might have seemed foreign to a West Coast guy, but Vermeil embraced the opportunity with open arms. More importantly, he knew that he had not been brought in because he was telegenic; he understood that it was his responsibility to turn around the fortunes of what had become a very sad team.

Vermeil worked tirelessly to do just that. He became one of the first coaches known for putting in 18-hour days. The long hours paid off. Vermeil proved to be an excellent strategist with a natural ability to find and exploit the best matchups on the team. However, his greatest strengths were his organizational skills and his ability to work with others.

Vermeil made every second count on the practice field, and he was not shy about pushing his players to the limit. He also proved to be a great communicator who knew what to say and when to listen. Despite earning the nickname "The Little Dictator," Vermeil won great loyalty from his players because they realized how much he cared about his job. Vermeil was known for his tendency to cry during emotional situations while he was coaching in St. Louis and Kansas City, but those tears were more likely to come from the players during his first years in Philadelphia. He drove his players relentlessly in an effort to beat the losing mentality out of them. It took a couple of years, but it worked.

The Eagles struggled in Vermeil's first season and ended the year with a 4–10 record in 1976. The wins and losses were the same as they had been the year before under McCormack, but everything else was different. Vermeil was sharp, organized, demanding, and optimistic. He introduced himself to the team by announcing open tryouts at the Vet, an idea that would eventually result in the signing of a 30-year-old rookie named Vince Papale, who would go on to become a special teams demon. Papale's improbable run resulted in a feature film about his life 30 years later, but at the time it sent a message to the team that nobody's job was secure unless they were productive.

Vermeil knew he made life tough on his players, but he did it with a purpose. "I demand a lot from people," Vermeil said. "I keep people who want to give something. It's not hard to motivate when you surround yourself with people who want the same thing you do."

The Eagles were 5–9 in 1977, but the one-game improvement in their record did not reflect what was going on in the locker room. The Eagles were becoming a tighter and better team. Vermeil found a true quarterback in the strong-armed Ron Jaworski, who warmed to the task of leading the offense and making gutsy throws. The defense was also getting better—and nastier—as the season progressed. They never gave up more than 23 points per game during the season.

The final game of 1977 finally convinced the Eagles that they could be a great team. They were playing a lousy New York Jets team that had won only three games, and the Eagles were confident of finishing the season on a strong note. They did just that in a 27–0 win that marked the first start of running back Wilbert Montgomery's career. He ran for 103 yards and two touchdowns. Vermeil realized he had a one-two punch he could count on, and he couldn't wait for the next season to begin.

The Eagles made significant progress in 1978, earning a 9–7 record—their first winning season since 1966. They made the playoffs as a wild-card team before dropping a heartbreaking 14–13 game to the Falcons. Montgomery established himself as one of the best running backs in the league with a 1,220-yard season, becoming the first Eagles running back to surpass 1,000 yards since Steve Van Buren ran for 1,146 yards in 1949.

The Eagles proved to be a resilient team with a number of unusual ways to win games. One of their most famous victories was a 19–17 win over the Giants on the road when New York attempted to run out the clock with a 17–12 lead. Instead, Giants quarterback Joe Pisarcik botched a handoff to running back Larry Csonka; Eagles defensive back Herman Edwards picked up the bouncing ball and ran 26 yards into the end zone to complete the famous "Miracle of the Meadowlands" victory.

The Eagles added a 10–3 win over Green Bay to their record, a game in which backup quarterback John Sciarra—a former Vermeil star at UCLA—scored on an option play to give the Eagles the margin of victory. The team also exorcised some demons with a 14–10 win at St. Louis, their first victory over the Cardinals in nine tries.

Vermeil knew his team was ready to make a real run in 1979. His first three years had showed him how much a team could improve with enhanced talent and a dedication to hustle, and the arrival of Marion Campbell as the defensive coordinator in 1977 had turned the Eagles defense into a finely tuned machine. "The Swamp Fox," as Campbell was known, had been a star on the 1960 championship team, and had since honed his coaching skills in stints with the Patriots, Vikings, Rams, and Falcons. Campbell's experience as a player and coach in the pro game gave Vermeil quite a bit of comfort.

Prior to the 1979 season, Vermeil next brought in another experienced hand, Sid Gillman, to lead the offense. Gillman is clearly among the most significant contributors to the development of the offensive game in the modern NFL. Many head coaches would be intimidated by the presence of such strong coordinators as Gillman and Campbell, but Vermeil viewed them as key lieutenants in his army.

"One of my weaknesses is a lack of depth in the background of pro football," Vermeil said after hiring Gillman. "The people who have been in the game for years have a depth of thinking that I can't have yet based on the experience that these people have.

"Adding a Sid Gillman to my staff helps me in that area. It gives a depth in offensive thinking. It will give us the advantage of not getting too stereotyped in the way we attack.

"I surround myself with strong assistants like Sid Gillman and Marion Campbell, but it works because I am not afraid to give orders. I have had problems delegating, but I am getting better. It's just that when you are building a program, you feel the responsibility to do everything yourself. That may be a lack of security on my part, but I've always felt if you want the job done right, you have to do it yourself."

The 1979 season brought even more success and a continued climb up the NFL ladder for the Eagles. They started the year with six wins in their first seven games, but hit a bump in the road when they lost three consecutive contests, at Washington, Cincinnati, and at home against Cleveland. Panic was starting to set in prior to their next game, a Monday nighter in Dallas.

The Eagles had never won a game at Texas Stadium, and most of the experts were predicting that they would be eviscerated by their longtime rivals. Instead, the Eagles came out with a razor-sharp game in which they spotted the Cowboys a 7–0 lead and then scored the next 24 points to seize control of the game. Jaworski threw two touchdown passes to Harold Carmichael and barefoot kicker Tony Franklin blasted a 59-yard field goal. After the Cowboys drew within three points at 24–21, Montgomery put the game away with a 37-yard fourth-quarter touchdown run.

Vermeil had won over the team and its owner before that game, but the win in Dallas convinced all the doubters in Philadelphia and throughout the league that the Eagles would be a force to be reckoned with for as long as Vermeil remained in charge. He was tough, demanding, and at times unforgiving. But he was totally dedicated to his team and the job and he was bringing about dramatic improvements.

The one thing that made Vermeil different from other taskmaster-type coaches was the strong emotional bond he developed with his players. He may have worked them like dogs, but he loved them, too. Vermeil hugged his players in pregame warm-ups, wished them luck, and told them about the opportunities that were in front of them. He would frequently tear up in his pregame speeches, an emotion that would have been deemed laughable or phony coming from any other coach. But with Vermeil, it was clearly legitimate.

"Dick has always cared about his players," Jaworski said. "It's never been an act, and it is a part of his makeup. When you see him hugging players and smiling at them, that's because there is a lot of love there. He has real emotion and that's just the kind of person he is."

The win over Dallas reignited the Eagles, and they closed the regular season with five wins in their last six games. They tied the Cowboys for first in the NFC East with an 11–5 record, but were relegated to the wild-card spot because Dallas had a superior conference record (10–2 versus 9–3). They won their first playoff game, punishing the Chicago Bears 27–17, in their first playoff victory since the 1960 NFL Championship game over

Green Bay. The Eagles played poorly in the first half and trailed 17–10 at halftime, leaving the field to a chorus of boos. But Jaworski threw two touchdown passes in the second half to lead the Eagles to the win.

Many thought the Eagles were on their way to the NFC Championship game when they drew the Tampa Bay Bucs in the divisional playoffs. Tampa Bay had a nasty defense led by great defensive end Lee Roy Selmon; however, their offense was suspect. But the Eagles didn't play with the fire they had had throughout the rest of the season. The game was not as close as the 24–17 score would seem to indicate.

Gary Smith of *The Philadelphia Inquirer* said the Eagles never had a chance. "They came out dead and stayed that way," Smith wrote. "They should have lost by three touchdowns."

There were whispers that Vermeil had overworked his team and that they had nothing left in the tank by the time they played the Bucs. But that theory only fueled Vermeil's fire. His camp prior to the start of the 1980 season was as tough as ever. The last thing he wanted to hear was anybody complaining about being over-worked. "If anybody uses being tired as an excuse for losing, then I will find somebody to play their position who isn't tired," said Vermeil at the team's West Chester, Pennsylvania, training camp. "They had better not use that as an excuse. We're not changing. This has nothing to do with losing to Tampa Bay last year. If we had won that game, everyone would have said it would have been because we outworked them. That's the way we do things and we are not going to change."

The pain of losing to Tampa Bay in the postseason and the toughness of the 1980 training camp steeled the Eagles even further. They rolled through their schedule, clearly looking like one of the league's dominant teams as they won 11 of their first 12 games. But eyebrows were raised when they dropped three of their last four contests. A 35–27 defeat at Dallas in the regular-season finale had no impact on the Eagles' status as the number one team in the NFC, but still, it left a bad taste in their mouths. Carmichael had failed to catch a pass for the first time in 127 games, and besides, it was a loss to the hated Cowboys.

The Eagles were heavily favored over the Vikings in their divisional playoff game. They had rolled to a 42–7 win at Minnesota in the second week of the season, and now they were rested and ready for a game at home. Another rout was expected. Defying those expectations, the Vikings went out to a 14–0 lead, and there was legitimate fear in the stands—if not on the sideline. Montgomery was struggling with some nagging injuries and the defense was playing far below their usual standards.

The normally mild-mannered Campbell lit into his defensive players at half time, and they responded in the second half by recovering three Viking fumbles and coming up with five interceptions. Jaworski, Carmichael, and Montgomery also came alive in the second half as the Eagles rolled to a 31–16 win.

Nobody was more impressed by the Eagles' second-half performance than venerable Viking head coach Bud Grant. "That's a very good team over there," Grant said. "They played their best football in the second half, and that's when good teams play well. They have a lot of talent, they put it on display when the game was on the line, and they are no fluke."

Vermeil was very concerned about injuries to Montgomery and his receivers as the team got ready for the NFC Championship game against the Cowboys. Vermeil fired a shot prior to the game, informing the league that his team would wear white at home, forcing the Cowboys to wear their blue jerseys—something that Tom Landry and general manager Tex Schramm considered bad luck. Vermeil was looking for any edge he could get; he was sick of hearing the Cowboys described as America's Team. He was determined to make everything about their trip to the Vet, a place they despised, as uncomfortable as possible.

The elements were in the Eagles favor: the game was played in minus-17 windchill conditions. But Vermeil's team had a lot more going for it than the color of their uniforms and the weather. Montgomery opened the game with a 42-yard touchdown run; the Eagles then proceeded to punish the Cowboys from the opening kickoff to the final gun. The Eagles executed the perfect marriage of strategy and physical football; the Cowboys were beaten far more decisively than the 20-7 score indicates. Montgomery's early touchdown, which came with the Cowboys' nickel defense on the field, was the result of some superbly timed blocks paired with Montgomery's shocking speed.

The fans roared their approval throughout the game and then danced onto the field at the final gun as they realized they were going to the Super Bowl. A few hours later, they learned they would play the Oakland Raiders, a team they had defeated in November. While there were a lot of hurdles to overcome, the Eagles were overjoyed to be two weeks away from playing in their very first Super Bowl.

That game did not go according to the script, as the loose and rowdy Raiders beat the uptight and over-prepared Eagles 27–10. Vermeil was crushed by the defeat. He was gracious after the game, crediting the Raiders with an outstanding game plan and execution, but the loss was difficult for him to live with.

The Eagles seemed to suffer a post–Super Bowl hangover in 1981. They played well and went to the playoffs again after finishing 10–6, but the team lost momentum after midseason. They had started with a 6–0 mark, but then lost six of their final 10. Their swagger and persona seemed diminished. When they dropped a 27–21 contest to the Giants in the wild-card game after falling behind 20–0, the frustration in the locker room and the coach's office was palpable.

The Eagles played poorly in 1982, unable to find their rhythm in the strike-torn season. They won only three of nine games. Vermeil was simply worn out, and finally he decided that he had had enough. He went on to coin a phrase that would cut across all levels of American society when he announced his resignation: "I am emotionally burned out," Vermeil said. "I need a break from coaching."

Vermeil turned over the reins of the team he loved to Campbell, leaving pro football behind for the relative tranquility of life at home with his wife Carol, as well as some time spent behind the microphone.

Vermeil left Philadelphia without the championship he wanted so badly, but he had established himself as the most beloved and respected coach in team history. In a town as demanding as Philadelphia, that's a major accomplishment.

THE VERMEIL RESIGNATION

It had been enough. The intensity. The demands on his time. The frustration of coming close but never quite getting there. Vermeil knew there had to be a better way—a chance to taste some of life's more delicious moments.

The frustration of losing Super Bowl XV to the Raiders never left Vermeil or his players. They were still a good team in 1981; they made the playoffs and had some good moments, mostly during a 6–0 start. But there was none of the anticipation and joie de vivre that the team had enjoyed during its rollicking roll through the 1980 season.

The playoff loss was particularly painful. The Eagles faced an up-and-coming New York Giants team with steely eyed head coach Ray Perkins on the sideline; Perkins in turn entrusted his strong crew of linebackers to emerging leader Bill Parcells. Parcells's group included the league's most fearsome player since Dick Butkus in his prime—Lawrence Taylor, a source of nightmares and sleepless nights for quarterbacks throughout his Hall of Fame career. And no quarterback was as tormented by Taylor as Jaworski.

The Giants were coming off the high of beating the Dallas Cowboys in overtime to qualify for the playoffs in the last game of the season. The Eagles were expected to dust off these upstarts with about as much difficulty as swatting a mosquito on a summer evening.

But sometimes the mosquito takes a little bite before it gets swatted. That's just what happened to the Eagles when the Giants jumped to a 20–0 lead in the first quarter. The Eagles played on more even terms after that quick start, but the Giants hung on to win 27–21.

During the course of the 1981 season, Vermeil found himself in the grip of an emotional strain that was beginning to take a toll. He was as intense as ever, but he wasn't getting any joy from the kinds of moments that had meant so much to him in previous years. Players and assistants could see that his demeanor had changed and that he was no longer enjoying an occupation that he had once loved to his core.

Vermeil often found himself watching game film—watching a play, reversing the film, watching the play again, and repeating the process—but instead of studying the film and picking apart his opponents' weaknesses for his team to exploit, his mind was vacant. He later admitted to being frozen with fear.

The 1982 season brought an unexpected respite. Vermeil was just as tired and worn out during training camp and the start of the season as he had been in the late part of 1981, but the NFL players went on strike after three games. The battle between the league and the National Football League Players Association (NFLPA) shut down the game for two months. Forced to take time off, Vermeil had a chance to breathe again. He took drives with his wife and noticed things like fall colors, Sunday brunch, and going to bed at a normal hour without three tons of stress on his shoulders. He spent time with his family—and enjoyed it.

When the strike ended, it was back to the grind for Vermeil—and his team was not responding. The Eagles never found their rhythm in 1982, finishing last in the NFC East with a 3–6 record. The final game was a 26–24 loss to the Giants.

Despite having three years left on a contract that would have paid him $250,000 per year, Vermeil decided he had had enough—although he had a difficult time coming to that decision. He asked his wife to choose whether he should stay or go, and she told him that if he couldn't decide for himself, he didn't need to stay with the job any longer.

Said Vermeil after announcing his decision: "I need a break from coaching, to get out for a while. I want to see if I can live without it. If I can't, I will work my way back to football."

Vermeil told reporters at his resignation press conference that he had a flaw in his personality that accelerated his burn out. "I can't turn off responsibilities," Vermeil said. "I've been in coaching 23 years with this kind of personality. It has gradually caught up to me. It's time to take a break from coaching. If I get back into it, the only negative is that it won't be in Philadelphia."

He became emotional when he talked about the players he had coached through the years—men who had given their all for the Eagles and made them a legitimate franchise again after the team's nearly two-decade dormancy.

"I love these people and I hope my players understand," Vermeil explained. "It's not easy, saying good-bye. But as a professional, I owe it to them and I owe it to myself."

Vermeil turned the team over to his trusted defensive coordinator, Campbell. "He is going to be missed," Campbell said. "These words will never come out of his mouth, but he is a great coach."

Vermeil went into broadcasting and became one of the top college football analysts in the game. While it seemed at first that coaching was out of his blood after more than 15 years on the sideline, he surprised the football world by returning to the NFL in 1997 as head coach of the St. Louis Rams.

When he returned to the league, Vermeil was hungry once again and also a bit wiser. While he still drove his team hard and forced them to endure tough practices, he had learned when to back off. Two years later, the Rams beat the Tennessee Titans 23–16 in Super Bowl XXXIV. The victory was clinched when St. Louis linebacker Mike Jones tackled Tennessee wide receiver Kevin Dyson on the 1-yard line.

As Vermeil praised his players and thanked everyone he could think of, he also remembered his former players with the Eagles who had come so far with him. "I am thinking of all of them right now and I hope they know that at least a little piece of this victory is for them," Vermeil said.

The words touched his former players. "To think that he would say something like that about players he had coached so long ago," said Eagles tight end John Spagnola. "It was very touching—and typical of Dick Vermeil."

BUDDYBALL

Love him or hate him, Buddy Ryan was clearly an original in a league that has far too many copycats.

Ryan is best known as the Eagles head coach from 1986 through 1990 and as the defensive coordinator of the 1985 Super Bowl Champion Chicago Bears, but he started as an assistant coach with the New York Jets in the 1960s and was also part of the

Weeb Ewbank defensive brain trust that engineered the most famous upset in the history of the game.

Joe Namath may have got all the headlines for "guaranteeing" that the American Football League would win the Super Bowl in 1968, but it was defensive coordinator Walt Michaels and assistant coach Ryan who put together the game plan that neutralized the powerful Colts offense.

The decision for the Jets to drop its linebackers and commit to complex coverage schemes was Ryan's idea; using that plan, the Jets forced five turnovers (four interceptions and one fumble recovery), which kept the Colts from establishing any offensive rhythm. "We had a bad day, and there's no doubt about that," said Colts quarterback Earl Morrall. "But they showed us things we had never seen in the NFL."

Ryan's time with the Jets and Ewbank was the key influence on his decision to make pressure the focal point of every defense he ever coached. Ewbank was much more of an offensive innovator than a defensive specialist, but he did everything in his power to keep quarterback Namath upright and able to step into his throws.

"Weeb said he would do anything to protect the quarterback, even if it meant keeping nine men in to help," Ryan explained. "That's when I figured if it was that important to Weeb to protect the quarterback, then it ought to mean just as much to the defense to get him, even if it meant sending in nine.

"The other thing Weeb said was tough for him was going against mixed coverages. Now here was a guy who was about a hundred years ahead of his time in offensive philosophy. I thought, hell, if it's that tough on Weeb, then if I ever get the chance to head up a defense, that's what I'll use." Ryan brought his defensive creativity with him when he became the defensive coordinator of the powerful Minnesota Vikings in the mid-1970s. While the Jets had a group of hard-working, intelligent players with only average athletic ability, the Vikings were gifted with quickness, speed, strength, and a tough defense. Ryan pushed great players to become even greater, and his Purple People Eaters squad became one of the best defensive units to ever take the field in the NFL.

Ryan was brought into the Minnesota organization by general

Getty Images

Despite his demanding and quirkish personality, Eagle players always sold out for Buddy Ryan.

manager Jim Finks; when Finks moved into a similar position with the Bears, he hired Ryan in Chicago in 1978. The Bears defenses showed steady improvement, often playing with a savage attitude, and owner George Halas took notice. He fired head coach Neill Armstrong in 1982, but he made sure that Ryan stayed. That didn't sit well with new head coach Mike Ditka—he and Ryan were about as comfortable together as iodine on a fresh scrape—but they managed to forge a partnership in order to build a great championship team.

The 1985 Bears turned Ryan into a household name, and he was hired by Eagles owner Norman Braman to turn things around in Philadelphia in 1986. Ryan was more than ready for the challenge. He had spent 25 years as an assistant coach in college and pro football, and was 51 years old, when he took the reins.

All Ryan cared about was building a winning team. He was uninterested in the public relations side of football—even though that was a big part of what had helped the NFL grow into the most powerful sports league in the world. It wasn't that Ryan didn't enjoy the give-and-take with the media; it was just that he was not about to feed writers and broadcasters with easy explanations or coddle them with quips.

"Some people go out of their way to look good in public and always say and do the right things," Ryan said. "They want to maintain an image. To me that's phony and mealymouthed. I'm not someone who is going to whine and cry. That isn't my style and it never was." As a result, Ryan said and did whatever he had on his mind. When he came to Philadelphia, it was assumed he would turn to Earnest Jackson to run the football. Jackson had run for more than 1,000 yards in the previous two seasons (with the Chargers in '84 and then with the Eagles in '85). However, Ryan didn't like Jackson's style, work ethic, or speed, so he cut him from training camp before the start of the season.

Did Ryan cushion the blow for Jackson by thanking him for what he had done or wishing him well in his career? No chance— that was not the way Ryan did things. "Why did I cut him? I'll tell you why. He wasn't worth a damn. If we could have gotten something for him, we would have traded him. But he wasn't worth a bag of footballs or a cold six-pack." Ryan began his head coaching career with a 5–10–1 record, but he was rebuilding and motivating the team for the very solid run that was about to come. He had 20 new players. He wanted to build an attacking defense similar to the one he had had in Chicago, although he was also willing to have a few big-play specialists like quarterback Randall Cunningham and tight end Keith Jackson to lead the offense.

While Ryan was a coach who wouldn't accept excuses or failure, he did realize that building a team was a process; turning a team around wasn't going to happen immediately. The one thing he wanted to do in his first season was get his players to buy into his system and believe that they had a coach who was capable of turning the team around. From that perspective, he thought his first season was a success.

"I think the players believe in what we are doing," Ryan said as he began his second season in Philadelphia. "They know we're going to get there and that it's just a matter of maturing together. We put together a nucleus of a team and now we build it. We went through growing pains, but that's going to happen when you start seven or eight rookies. Young players don't know how to win. But once they understand, watch out."

The Eagles came together in the 1987 season. They finished with a 7–8 record, but that was the season that the NFL used replacement players during the strike. While many head coaches around the league were supportive of the move in hopes that it would break the players union, Ryan won undying loyalty from his striking players when he ripped the replacements as the "worst football players I've ever seen." The Eagles lost all three of their replacement games, but when the regulars came back, the team had an impenetrable bond that would pay dividends during the next three seasons.

Naturally, Ryan's defensive unit was the first aspect of the team to assert its will. Philadelphia developed a nasty, hard-hitting, and punishing defense. As that unit grew in stature, Eagles fans started to take on an even more aggressive personality as well. The fans in the Oakland Coliseum have a reputation for being intimidating, and a dog-faced "Big John" character leads a crew of Cleveland canines at Browns Stadium, but no group of fans has ever had a greater impact than Eagles fans—especially during the Ryan era.

It was an open secret around the league that Ryan had offered his players bonus money if they could knock a key player out of a game with a big hit. That kind of bounty hunting helped make the Eagles more vicious and their fans more rowdy.

When the Cardinals came to Philadelphia in 1988, fans threw a container of salsa on wide receiver J.T. Smith. While that may sound tame and almost laughable, Smith would not agree. "All that pepper burned my eyes," he told *The Arizona Republic.* "The guy threw stuff out of a container. I wanted to go up there and hit the guy with my helmet. If you are going to throw stuff at players, you might as well be a man and come down on the field and do it."

At the same time that Smith was having trouble with the fans in the stands, Cardinals special teamer Ron Wolfley was having his own problems on the field. Wolfley accused Eagles player John Klingel of grabbing him in the groin area in an attempt to injure him. "I thought Houston was dirty," Wolfley said. "But [Houston Oiler coach] Jerry Glanville's team looks like a church choir compared to these guys. They are flat-out dirty.

"A guy [Klingel] jumped on me and grabbed a groin-full. I know his number and I know who he is. They are cheap women. That's all right, because they are coming back to our place. It will be ground zero."

Eagles defensive back Andre Waters was the poster boy for dirty play. He went after Rams quarterback Jim Everett and was fined $1,500 for it. He threatened and battled Redskin quarterback Doug Williams, and he dove at the knees and ankles of countless other players. Waters was regularly described as the "most hated player in the league." But not by Ryan. He loved Waters and the intimidation level he brought to the team. Ryan knew that if opponents were thinking about avoiding serious injuries and protecting themselves, they would not be able to concentrate fully on winning the game.

It wasn't pretty, but it certainly was the Ryan way of doing things. He wanted players who could walk it and talk it when it came to toughness and all-around play on the field. "We bring young kids in here who are cocky and arrogant," Ryan said. "They don't stare at the ground and kick rocks when they talk to you. They believe in themselves and they believe in our team. That's why we are going to have one hell of a football team."

Ryan's team showed dramatic improvement, and the Eagles made the playoffs in 1988, '89, and '90. But they never made it far in the playoffs, losing to the Bears in '88, the Rams in '89, and the Redskins in '90. Ryan could build a team and get emotional play on a consistent basis, but when it came to rallying his players when the season was on the line, something was missing.

He also earned the enmity of coaches and media people throughout the league. In the famous Bounty Bowl against the Cowboys on Thanksgiving Day in 1989, word filtered to the Cowboys sideline that Ryan had offered to pay his players extra if they took out Cowboys quarterback Troy Aikman or place-kicker Luis Zendejas. Dallas coach Jimmy Johnson was livid; he wanted to confront Ryan in the middle of the field after the game. But Ryan had never followed the tradition of shaking hands with the opposing coach after the game. He followed his team into the locker room instead. "I wanted to say something to Buddy," Johnson barked after the game. "But he wouldn't stay on the field long enough. He took his big, fat butt into the tunnel."

Much of the media labeled Ryan as an insecure coach who wanted to turn his players into bullies as an extension of his own personality.

Meanwhile Eagles owner Braman was growing tired of Ryan's smart-aleck remarks and his pride in a team that lived on the edge. The 20–6 playoff loss to Washington and Joe Gibbs was more than Braman could endure. He fired Ryan despite his three straight playoff appearances.

There was not an iota of regret in Ryan's voice when he spoke publicly after the dismissal. "I've been fired before for losing," Ryan said. "But I've never been fired for winning. It's their loss and my gain."

Ryan took two years off from football before emerging as the defensive coordinator for Jack Pardee in Houston. He helped the

Oilers build a playoff-worthy defense, but Ryan made headlines again when he cracked Oilers offensive coordinator Kevin Gilbride with a right cross to the jaw because Ryan didn't like Gilbride's play calling. Nobody argued that Ryan did not have a point, but the way he handled his anger was clearly inappropriate.

Nevertheless, the Arizona Cardinals hired him to be their head coach prior to the 1994 season. The moribund Cardinals had had little talent and almost no success since moving to the desert from St. Louis following the 1987 season. But that did not stop Ryan from telling everyone that he would turn things around. "You've got a winner in town," boasted Ryan. Despite his big talk, the Cardinals finished only 8–8 his first season before going in the tank with a 4–12 record the following year. Ryan barely knew his players' names, usually referring to them by their numbers. His act wore thin, and he was fired.

Ryan's ability to build, lead, and coach a defense was never in question during his coaching career. But in the end, his arrogance, temper, and lack of tact proved to be his undoing.

THE RYAN-DITKA FEUD

The Philadelphia Eagles began playing football in the NFL in 1933, and they have since played the Chicago Bears 38 times, including three times in the playoffs. Given the amount of time the two teams have been in existence—the Bears started way back in 1920—they have not played that many games against each other, and the rivalry between them has not been particularly heated.

For instance, nobody in Philadelphia would confuse the Eagles-Bears rivalry with their wars against the Redskins, the Cowboys, or the Giants. In Chicago, the thought of the two teams getting together doesn't have the same impact as a Bears-Vikings game and doesn't even come close to the feelings stirred up by the ancient Chicago–Green Bay rivalry. However, during a four-year period between 1986 and 1989, no two teams had more hate for each other than the Bears and the Birds.

It would probably be more accurate to say that no two coaches had more animus between them then the Eagles' Ryan and the Bears' Ditka.

Ryan began his Bears career as defensive coordinator after being brought on by legendary owner Halas and head coach Armstrong for the 1978 season. Following Armstrong's firing in 1981, many players and staffers thought Ryan would make an outstanding head coach. Defensive tackle Allen Page even wrote a letter to Halas imploring the aging owner to retain Ryan. The letter was signed by all of Chicago's defensive players.

As tensions regarding the identity of the new head coach swirled, Halas was driven in a golf cart to address the defense on the practice field. According to a 1988 article by the *Chicago Tribune*'s Don Pierson, Halas inadvertently stirred the pot when he told the players that "Buddy Parker is a fine coach; you have nothing to worry about."

Halas signed Ryan to a new deal as defensive coordinator shortly before hiring Ditka as head coach. The two strong-willed personalities began to butt heads almost immediately, even though the Chicago defense was playing lights out. The Bears dominated the league in all defensive categories, though the team struggled to win games in 1982 and '83. Ditka had his own ideas about what he wanted from his defense—he loved the 3-4 scheme—but he allowed Ryan to have full control because the unit was so effective. Safety Dave Duerson said that Ditka only interfered in a defensive meeting once and that Ryan told him to get out, saying, "This is my team; these are my players."

The intense dislike between the two came to a head during the Bears' only loss in 1985. Playing the highest-rated Monday night game in the history of the series, Dan Marino and the Dolphins strafed the Bears' impenetrable defense. At halftime, Ditka and Ryan nearly came to blows when the defensive coordinator told the head coach to have a cornerback cover Dolphin wideout Nat Moore instead of using punishing linebacker Wilber Marshall.

Ditka offered Ryan the opportunity to take their dispute outside the locker room. "We can do it any way you want to. We can go right out back and get it on or you can shape your ass up," Ditka later recalled saying. But no fight ensued, and after that loss, the Bears never come close to losing again as they marched to their Super Bowl XX win over New England.

The night before that game, Ryan informed his defensive players that he was leaving after the game to become head coach of the Eagles. "But no matter where I go," Ryan said, "you guys will always be my heroes." Ryan and his charges cried like babies until Steve McMichael threw a chair that wound up stuck in the chalkboard. The team roared out of the meeting room imbued with the thought of giving Ryan a going-away present.

The Patriots never stood a chance. They were battered into submission in the Superdome. The 46–10 win was the biggest margin of victory in Super Bowl history at that time.

After Ryan left Chicago, the Eagles-Bears rivalry had a place in the national consciousness. The first matchup between Ryan and Ditka came at Soldier Field in week two of the 1986 season. Ditka remained diplomatic when the media questioned him on his reunion with his former assistant. "I don't have a psychiatric degree, so if you guys want to talk football, we can talk. The other guy was here last year, but he's not here anymore," Ditka told reporters.

Ryan, on the other hand, didn't see fit to muzzle himself. He told one publication that the Bears "didn't have a chance" to repeat as world champions. "Any team that won the year before has a tough time," Ryan explained. "You just can't do it. Too many things have to go right for you."

McMichael was not pleased with his old coach's assessment, saying, "The old fat man has been talking a little shit in Philly, hasn't he?"

Meanwhile, Eagles backup running back Mike Waters was running his mouth too, calling the Bears "pansies" and "babies" prior to the game—which Chicago won in overtime, 13–10, on a Kevin Butler field goal.

The following season Chicago and Philadelphia met again, this time in Veteran's Stadium. The two coaches kept relatively quiet, perhaps because this was the first game to be played after the NFLPA called its strike. The replacement players took the field in relative peace. The two coaches took opposing views on the strike. Ditka embraced the replacement players as "the real Bears," while Ryan called his team "the worst bunch of football players I've ever seen."

Philadelphia's AFL-CIO contingent threatened a disturbance at the game, and the Teamsters circled the field with semi trucks. The Bears players arrived at 5:00 AM to avoid any hassle, and only 4,000 fans showed up—perhaps because they were afraid of trouble or perhaps because no one was interested in seeing two replacement squads square off. The "Spare Bears" rolled to a 35–3 win.

The teams didn't meet during the 1988 regular season, but they did come face-to-face in the playoffs. The Eagles had taken the NFC by surprise, winning the East with a 10–6 record, their first winning season since 1981. Meanwhile Chicago had rebounded from key personnel losses, injuries, and Ditka's heart attack, compiling a 12–4 record and securing home-field advantage throughout the playoffs.

It seemed like a match made by the football gods when the Eagles and the Bears met in a divisional playoff game at Solider Field on December 31. Ditka pretended to take the high road when asked about Ryan, calling the matchup just another game. "Our team will play their team. I doubt that he will make any tackles, or I will make any catches. Team against team, that's what it will be," Ditka said. But don't think for a minute that the prickly Ditka liked the idea of losing a playoff game to his former assistant.

As usual, Ryan made no attempt at diplomacy—something that is sometimes an admirable trait in the politically correct NFL. He called the Eagles' personnel "better than the Bears at every position except middle linebacker," a nod to future Hall of Famer Mike Singletary. Ryan also said that it was really the Eagles who had home-field advantage in Chicago, since he had never lost a playoff game there—unlike Ditka.

Adding to the verbal barrage was former Bear safety Todd Bell, who had moved on to play weak-side linebacker for Ryan. Bell was fired up before, during, and after the game, taunting Bears players and criticizing Ditka and the Bears' organization for the way he had been treated in Chicago.

By the time the actual game got started, the temperature was unseasonably warm in Chicago. The Bears opened up a 17–9 lead on Ryan and the Eagles when a sudden fog descended upon the field. Fans at Soldier Field couldn't see the game, and players couldn't see more than three or four yards in front of them.

The Bears held on to win even though the Eagles moved the ball with ease, penetrating Chicago's 25-yard line nine times. The disappointed Ryan was brave as he met the media, giving credit to the Bears' defense—but not their coaching. "Credit the Bears," he told his players. "But hold your heads high."

In the Monday night meeting between the two teams in 1989, the Soldier Field crowd no longer felt any kinship for Ryan—and let him know it with catcalls and insulting banners. The Eagles defense was joined on the field by another Bears castoff, Al Harris, and Bell again showed his grudge against Chicago by getting into a heated argument with Richard Dent. (Bell broke his leg in the contest.)

Chicago won this matchup 27–13 even though Eagles quarterback Randall Cunningham threw for 401 yards. After the game, Ryan said, "You don't lose that many times to anyone and stay in this league long."

Ditka hit back at Ryan for firing shots and taking a superior attitude. "I'm the duck and it's like water off a duck's back," Ditka said. "He's just jealous. You know what they say. Empty tin cans make the most noise, and he's an empty tin can. This game is between the Bears and the Eagles, not Ditka and Ryan. We all know who would win that one. Ditka, hands down."

But it was Bears safety Shaun Gayle who said what most fans of the two teams, as well as the media, were now thinking: "Maybe what we could do after the game is all the players circle our cars in the parking lot and let the two of them have at it." What that fight might have looked like is something we'll have to leave up to our imaginations.

This emotional game may have taken something out of the Bears despite the fact that they walked away with the victory. Chicago held a 4–0 record after beating the Eagles but managed only two wins the rest of the way. They were never the same team for Ditka, and he was fired three years later.

Ryan's teams would finish 11–5, 10–6, and 10–6 from 1989 to 1991, but the outspoken coach was released after the 1991 season—and his winless playoff record and jarringly honest demeanor played big roles in his dismissal.

Ryan did ultimately manage to get a win over the Bears, but not with the Eagles—the victory came during the 1995 preseason, when Ryan was head coach of the Cardinals. Trailing 16–14 late in the final quarter, Ryan put his starters back in during the game's final minutes. The Cardinals starters, playing against men that would soon be cut, were able to move the ball down the field and secure the win with a late field goal. It may have been meaningless to everyone else, but the brazen old coach savored that one victory against his former club.

It was the only one he ever earned.

RICH KOTITE

Stumbling, bumbling, crumbling—he is the poster boy for poor coaching. Mention the name Rich Kotite and then start counting, and the guffaws and derisive laughter will start before you can reach the count of two.

Kotite cemented his losing image during a two-year stint with the Jets in the mid-1990s. However, if one wants to be fair about it, he actually did a decent job in Philadelphia after Buddy Ryan was fired in 1991.

Kotite was initially made to feel quite welcome by owner Braman. First of all, Braman loved Kotite just because he was not Buddy. While Ryan had been loved by his players, he was despised by the man who paid his salary. In almost every business, you have to give at least a modicum of respect to the man that signs the paychecks. But Ryan never even pretended to show respect for Braman. When the end finally came after yet another postseason defeat, Braman had to bite his lip to keep from smiling too broadly.

Kotite was an assistant on Ryan's staff prior to Braman's decision, and contrary to popular opinion, he was not stupid. While he did not openly campaign for the job, Kotite could see the handwriting on the wall. His goal was to build a team that would be respected throughout the league. "You look at the 49ers and it's hard not to have respect for the way they go about their business," Kotite said. "They are a classy team and they show good judgment. They just don't beat themselves. They play with consistency and there is no roller-coaster ride. That's what we want to establish here." But Kotite never came close to turning the Eagles into an organization like the 49ers of the mid-1990s.

Keith Byars, a mainstay during Ryan's run with the Eagles, said that Kotite did everything he could to do things differently than Ryan had. The Eagles had developed a reputation for being intimidators under Ryan's leadership, and Kotite wanted no part of that. He didn't believe in intimidating the opponent and creating fear or mayhem.

The problem, however, was that Kotite was unable to cultivate *any* kind of image or direction for his team. He was seen as a pawn of management and never did anything to create his own identity. It was difficult for players to take him seriously.

Kotite should have been able to impress his players. He had played tight end in the league, proving himself to be a tough guy who wouldn't back down on the field. He had been a boxer as a young man and had sparred with Muhammad Ali. He also had a booming voice that could be heard anywhere on the field during practice. He totally deserved the nickname "Bullhorn" that was thrust on him. But somehow, Kotite was unable to play the role of tough guy. He came across as something of a buffoon to his players.

While he had little ability to motivate or teach his players, Kotite's biggest weakness may have been his inability to judge talent. Draft choices Antone Davis, Siran Stacy, and Bernard Williams illustrated this weakness and ensured the team's downward spiral.

Kotite's inability to handle in-game decisions was another big part of the problem. Never was that more apparent than when he botched a decision on when to go for a two-point conversion against the Cowboys in 1994. The Eagles were trailing Dallas 24–7 late in the fourth quarter of a mid-October game at Texas Stadium when Eagles running back James Joseph busted loose on a 34-yard touchdown run with 5:27 remaining in the game, cutting the lead to 24-13. Kotite inexplicably decided to go for two points on the

Getty Images

Rich Kotite was reviled by the end of his tenure in Philadelphia in 1994 and is widely recognized as one of the worst head coaches in NFL history.

conversion, and later claimed he misread his chart (that says whether to go for one or two points on the extra point attempt) because of a water smudge.

The game was played in heavy rain and the footing was treacherous. Quarterback Cunningham was stopped short of the end zone, and the failed two-point conversion meant that the Eagles would still need two touchdowns to take the lead, instead of needing only a touchdown and field goal to tie the score.

"The rain smeared the ink," Kotite said glumly. Chart or no chart, smudge or no smudge, Kotite was roundly criticized for not recognizing what was an obvious blunder.

The Eagles did manage to win one playoff game during the Kotite regime, a dominating 36–20 win over the Saints in the 1992 wild-card round. The Eagles defense delivered superior play, and the offense did enough when it had the ball. But the Eagles were crushed by Dallas 34–10 the following week, and that would be the team's last postseason appearance under Kotite. The Eagles went from 11–5 in 1992 to 8–8 in '93 and 7–9 in '94.

Kotite had many problems as a head coach, but his inability to turn things around once they started to go wrong may have been his biggest problem. Nearly every NFL team will lose a couple of games in a row, but a good coach has the wherewithal to stop the bleeding. In 1993 the Eagles began the season with four straight wins; they also closed the year with a three-game winning streak. But in between those two streaks they lost eight out of nine games. They lost five straight games at home, an opportunity that gave Eagles fans plenty of time to let Kotite know how they felt about him.

In 1994 the Eagles appeared to right the ship, winning seven of nine and putting themselves in a position to challenge the Cowboys. But they were unable to sustain that success, dropping their last seven games. Included in that streak were losses to the Cardinals (coached by Ryan) and a season-ending 33–30 loss to the miserable Cincinnati Bengals (who were 3–13).

While Braman may at first have loved Kotite because he wasn't Ryan, that fact did not buy Kotite much security. The Eagles were sold to Jeffrey Lurie in 1994, and the new boss was not very happy with what he was seeing. Rumors abounded that Kotite would be dismissed at the end of the season, and his run in Philadelphia did in fact come to an end two days after that ignominious defeat in Cincinnati.

The Eagles had been significantly diminished during Kotite's four-year run. After starting off with one of the most powerful rosters in the league, they lost much of their swagger and were below average by the end of his reign.

P.T. Barnum's assertion that a sucker is born every minute was proven correct once again when Kotite was hired by the Jets after being let go by the Eagles. But if he was a disappointment in Philadelphia, he was an absolute joke in New York. He compiled a 4–28 record in two years, after he which he was sent packing, never to be heard from again in the world of professional football.

ANDY REID

The big man on the Eagles sideline cuts a memorable figure as he leads his team into battle. While owner Lurie was questioned intently when Andy Reid was hired in 1999 to succeed Ray Rhodes, the move has turned out to be the single most important hire in the team's recent past. He is the winningest coach in team history, surpassing greats like Greasy Neale and Vermeil with a hand so steady it would make a statue jealous. He has certainly proven himself able to create a game plan, execute it, follow through, and succeed. Reid has completely transformed the fortunes of the Eagles, turning the team into a model franchise after years of inconsistency.

Even though he had no experience as a head coach prior to being tapped by Lurie, Reid was well-prepared for the job after playing for the innovative LaVell Edwards at Brigham Young University. The Cougars had a dynamic team led by Jim McMahon; as an offensive tackle and guard, Reid faced a difficult battle every week. Offensive linemen are generally not as athletically gifted as the defensive linemen across the line of scrimmage. That's a fact of life in football that Reid recognized early in his career, and it helped him see clearly that there is a lot more to being a successful football player than winning the physical battle. He had to take advantage of his opponents mentally by getting them to play in a smaller area—therefore limiting the physical disadvantage.

While playing as a member of Edwards's explosive team in Utah, Reid met a young Cougar assistant coach named Mike Holmgren. The two not only resembled each other physically—at least in terms of build and walrus-like mustaches—but they also took an immediate liking to each other. Holmgren said that if he ever became a head coach, he would hire Reid as an assistant.

As a result of his time at Young, Reid spent as much time

By the time the Eagles hired Andy Reid in 1999, he had earned the right to be a head coach after a six-year apprenticeship in Green Bay under Mike Holmgren.

thinking about the game of football as he did playing it—he knew he had to gain a mental edge in order to have a chance. That mind-set made him a perfect coaching candidate; he understood the nuances of every position and the preparation each player had to undertake.

But more important than his technical understanding of the game, Reid also had a gift for understanding human nature. Nearly every successful leader understands that a steady hand, along with honest and forthright communication, gives an organization the best chance to succeed. But it can be difficult to stay on that path—to be honest and patient—when it's often easier to tell people what they want to hear and to change plans when success is not immediate. And it's even tougher to do it in the NFL, a business in which millions of individuals scrutinize and interpret your every maneuver and twitch on a daily basis.

Many NFL coaches have been done in by public opinion and criticism. Some succumb to the public's demand for change while others fight so hard to resist change that they lose sight of their original goal—winning. Reid has been able to resist that trap and has overcome many of the other obstacles that come with coaching in the NFL. Since the start of the 2000 season, he has built the steadiest team in the NFC; his success is due largely to the fact that he knows how to stay calm in every situation.

Lurie realized that Reid innately understood the principles of management, and those qualities have clearly served Reid well as the steward of the Eagle franchise. "He is like a CEO on the football field," Lurie said. "He understands the big picture and the short-term picture. You have to understand both. He is disciplined, prepared, and smart. That is a very good combination to have.

"He is a man who is very comfortable with himself. He has no ego. He's not paranoid about what others think or say. He's just a very genuine man." The business of coaching in the NFL is a very testing one, but Reid has proven himself at every turn. Although he is still working toward the goal of winning a Super Bowl, he has passed many other tests during the first nine years of his coaching career. After a tough 5–11 start in his initial season, the Eagles turned things around in 2000 with an 11–5 record and a win in the wild-card game against the Tampa Bay Bucs. The Eagles won the division title in each of the next three seasons, but seemingly hit a glass ceiling in the playoffs, with losses in each of the NFC Championship games. Frustration might have overtaken a lesser coach, but Reid has kept plugging away.

In 2004 Reid agreed to bring in talented but overbearing star wide receiver Terrell Owens to help the Eagles get to the promised land of the Super Bowl. Owens was a combative, egomaniacal individual who was nevertheless a great receiver with a gift for making big plays. The Eagles lacked a receiver of his abilities, so it was clear that this would be a good match—as long as Owens's outsized personality didn't tear the team apart.

Reid was prepared for the challenge, and the results that year were special. The Eagles won 13 of their first 14 games and rolled to the division title. In their fourth straight appearance in the NFC Championship game, Philadelphia handled Atlanta 27–10 and earned their shot at the Super Bowl in Jacksonville against the New England Patriots.

Owens, who had suffered an ankle injury late in the regular season and had missed the team's postseason wins over the Vikings and the Falcons, vowed that he would play in the Super Bowl—despite the fact that none of the Eagles medical personnel thought it was possible. His injury simply had not had enough time to heal sufficiently. But Reid never ruled him out, and when Owens proved on the practice field that he could run, cut, and catch the ball, Reid gave the receiver the opportunity he wanted.

The Eagles battled a great New England team for 60 minutes in Super Bowl XXXIX, finally losing 24–21. Quarterback Donovan McNabb rallied the team and had a good statistical game, but his play in the final minutes seemed erratic.

Owens criticized McNabb during the off-season, sowing the seeds for a disastrous 2005 season. Owens was also very unhappy with the contract that he had signed the previous season and demanded that the Eagles renegotiate. He dominated the headlines during the off-season and was a distraction when he came to training camp. Reid sent him home, where Owens attracted more attention by taking off his shirt and doing push-ups in his driveway.

With each garish "look at me" gesture, Owens turned off his teammates, the fans, and most importantly Reid. When he returned from his summertime suspension, it was clear that his attitude had not changed and it was just a matter of time before he was sent home again. Reid did not hesitate. Owens clearly had game-changing talent, but he was tearing apart the fabric of his team, and Reid decisively cut him.

After four straight division titles, the Eagles lost their way and went 6–10 in 2005. But the stumble was only temporary. They rebounded in 2006 with another NFC East title and a victory over the Giants in a wild-card game. They closed the year with a heartbreaking 27–24 loss to the Saints in the divisional playoffs. Still, it was an amazing season, not least of all because they achieved their record without McNabb, who had gone down with a serious injury for the second straight year. Reid brought in veteran Jeff Garcia as a backup, and even though most of the league questioned the move, the former 49ers Pro Bowler showed that he still had plenty left in his tank. It was a move that spoke of Reid's deft touch as a talent evaluator and a game planner. It demonstrated to his employers and Eagles fans that he was still the right man to lead their team.

Reid's success has come as no surprise to Holmgren, Reid's early mentor, who has been a dominant coach in the league himself with the Packers and the Seahawks. "There was never any question in my mind that Andy would become an outstanding coach," Holmgren said. "He had all the attributes a head coach needs and he's a clear thinker who makes outstanding decisions. What else do you want?"

WHEN THE FAT LADY SINGS

HERM'S MIRACLE IN THE MEADOWLANDS

"It ain't over 'til it's over."

Those immortal words were uttered by the New York Yankees' legendary catcher (and grammarian) Yogi Berra, when he was managing the New York Mets in 1973, when they went from last place in August to winning the National League pennant.

Another example of what can happen when a team plays with guts and determination when all appears to be lost occurred on November 19, 1978, when the Eagles went to Giants Stadium to play the Giants. What started off as a sleepy game between two ordinary teams would soon earn a permanent place in NFL lore as "The Miracle of the Meadowlands."

The Eagles came into the game with a 6–5 record, and Dick Vermeil had the team on track to produce what would be only its second winning season since 1962. The Giants had also been lethargic since their last NFL Championship game appearance in 1963, and they brought a three-game losing streak and a 5–6 record into this game.

New York played well enough to take a 17–12 lead into the final two minutes of the game. The Eagles had the ball, but a Ron Jaworski pass was intercepted with 1:23 remaining; all the Giants had to do to secure the victory was run out the clock. Jaworski—who had thrown three interceptions that day—was crestfallen and couldn't watch what he knew would happen next. Giants quarterback Joe Pisarcik would

Herman Edwards turned a fortuitous bounce in Giants Stadium into a franchise-defining moment for both the Eagles and the Giants before going on to a career as a head coach in the league.

take a knee and run out the clock. The Eagles had no timeouts left.

But Pisarcik did no such thing. Instead he gave the ball to fullback Larry Csonka, who powered up the middle for an 11-yard gain. Curious Giants fans looked at each other and wondered what was going on. Sure, the play was successful, but why risk exposing the ball?

On the next snap Pisarcik did what was expected, kneeling down after taking the snap from center Jim Clack. But before the officials could blow the whistle, Eagles linebacker Frank LeMaster knocked Clack backward and into Pisarcik.

Eagles defensive back Herman Edwards—who would later call the Meadowlands home during his five-year reign as head coach of the New York Jets from 2001 through 2005—recalled that the Giants were angry because a quarterback is not supposed to be hit when he is ending the game by taking a knee. Giants head coach John McVay was concerned that his team wasn't going to be able to protect Pisarcik, and he did not want to risk Pisarcik receiving an injury if he took a knee on what should have been the game's final play. "When LeMaster hit the center and Pisarcik got knocked down, a fight kind of started," Edwards said. "They got a little nervous about that because they figured maybe they'll get the quarterback hurt. So they called another run." McVay called for another handoff to Csonka, a play "that was put in on the first day of training camp."

The play was called in from the sideline; Pisarcik's call was met by quite a bit of protest in the New York huddle. But Pisarcik refused to change the call; he had changed a play in the previous week's game, and offensive coordinator Bob Gibson had threatened to replace him if he ever did it again.

As the Giants broke the huddle, New York running back Doug Kotar continued to jaw about the mini-fight that had ensued on the previous play. He told Edwards that the Giants were going to fall on the ball once more, and that he would see Edwards again in Philadelphia in a few weeks.

Or so he thought.

The Giants were just seconds away from a delay of game penalty when Clack readied to snap the ball. A penalty would have stopped the clock and given the Eagles another opportunity to tee off on Pisarcik. Clack snapped the ball early, and Pisarcik was not ready for it. He began to bobble the ball.

Here's how Edwards recalls what happened next: "Pisarcik tried to give the ball to Csonka, but because of the early snap, the timing was all messed up. I'm just kind of watching what's going, and I keep edging forward. Then I see the ball hit Csonka in the hip, and it's going to the ground. I just took off after that."

Edwards used a swim move to get by Kotar, who didn't realize what was happening and had no clue as to why Edwards was going full bore. "What are you doing?" asked a surprised Kotar.

The running back got his answer in less than a second. Edwards streaked into the backfield and was able to pick up the ball cleanly as it bounced off the spongy artificial turf. He was free and clear and ran 26 yards into the New York end zone for a touchdown. The play turned certain defeat into a 19–17 win. The Eagles had gone from misery to miracle in a matter of seconds.

Vermeil was beside himself with joy, but he refused to chalk up the victory to luck or circumstance. He credited his team's commitment to itself and defensive coordinator Marion Campbell. "Our defensive coordinator called an 11-man blitz," Vermeil said. "We hadn't given up. That's why our cornerback was in the backfield."

While his players may not have given up, Vermeil had actually started to walk to the Philadelphia locker room with his back to the field when he saw his own players jumping for joy and racing onto the field. He was taken aback for a second and couldn't understand what his players were celebrating. "What are you doing?" he shouted.

An instant later he understood.

The play had both immediate and long-term ramifications. The Eagles got an infusion of confidence and joy, and Vermeil was able to capitalize on the emotional moment to motivate his team. The Eagles went on to finish the year with a 9–7 record, earning a spot in the postseason.

"In our organization, it was probably a day that catapulted us to a different level," Edwards said. "At the time, we were struggling to win games, especially when we got to the end. But in this game, things broke the right way for us and we managed to win it. We were able to use the energy from the end of that game and propel ourselves into the playoffs."

The fruit of that victory came two years later when the Eagles became the dominant team in the NFC and made their first Super Bowl appearance. Their growth and confidence had been spurred by that fortuitous bounce in the Meadowlands.

Edwards had a reputation as a very solid and hard-working player before his memorable moment, and he became part of the NFL's

GIANT BLUES

The Eagles' miraculous "Miracle of the Meadowlands" victory stirred emotions in Philadelphia. Meanwhile, the Giants and their fans went into a state of deep depression after their nightmarish defeat.

New York went into the game with a reasonable hope of a winning season and an outside shot at the playoffs. Instead, they closed with a 6–10 mark and their third straight finish in the NFC East cellar. Offensive coordinator Gibson took the immediate fall and was fired the day after the loss, while the likable McVay was dismissed at the end of the season. That was the end of his NFL head coaching career, but McVay would go on to have a very successful run as general manager of the 49ers during their glory years.

That one famous play has had a long-term impact on McVay's psyche. "I still have about one nightmare a week because of that game," McVay recalled. "You never know what would have happened after that, but we had been pretty good. I think if that play hadn't happened, we probably would have had a winning season and could have made the playoffs."

McVay was viewed by the Giants management as a players' coach who allowed things to get a bit too comfortable in the locker room. After he was dismissed, they decided to borrow a page from the Eagles' book, going with Ray Perkins, a hard-nosed head coach like Vermeil.

But there was a huge difference between the two men. While Vermeil was tough and demanding, he was also very emotional about his players and the game. Down deep, everyone on the Eagles sideline knew that Vermeil loved them. Perkins was just the opposite. He never allowed his emotions to come to the surface and rarely, if ever, cracked a smile. He did, however, lead the Giants to a playoff appearance in 1981, their first since 1963, before he resigned at the end of the 1982 season to take the head coaching job at the University of Alabama. He was replaced by an unknown assistant named Bill Parcells, who would soon become a legend in his own right.

The miracle play has also had long-term ramifications for Pisarcik and Csonka. Pisarcik had actually been a major overachiever prior to that game and would have an eight-year career in the NFL—not too shabby for an undrafted, unknown free agent from New Mexico State University. His career with the Giants lasted for another year; he then ended his playing days with a five-year stint with the Eagles as a decent backup to Jaworski.

After leaving the Giants, Csonka finished his hall of fame career back with the Dolphins. He was a bruising fullback who could punish linebackers with his power and strength, and he was also quite nimble when he needed to be. Csonka was the MVP for the Dolphins in their Super Bowl VIII victory over the Vikings. He also had a memorable run in overtime that set up Garo Yepremian's game-winning field goal in a Christmas Day playoff win at Kansas City in 1971.

Csonka was a great player for one of the NFL's best teams of all time. However, when Eagles or Giants fans close their eyes and think of Csonka, the image that comes to mind is sure to be that botched handoff bouncing off his hip pad and into the arms of Edwards. One image doesn't necessarily ruin a career, but it sure can be difficult to shake.

legacy once glory had leaped into his arms and he ran to that improbable victory. "It's a funny deal," Edwards said. "I think players always want to be remembered for something, and I'm grateful that I am remembered for that. I tell my players all the time to play through the whistle and to finish the play. I insist on it because I've lived through it and seen what can happen when you live by that rule."

Even Yogi would have been amazed.

JAWS TO QUICK: 99 YARDS TO GLORY

Aptly named Eagles wide receiver Mike Quick was all about the big play, and the biggest play he ever made was perhaps the most famous regular-season overtime ending in NFL history.

It was the middle of the 1985 season, when the Eagles were getting bounced around by the Cowboys, Giants, and Redskins in the NFC East. The success of the Vermeil era was starting to become a distant memory, and the legendary Campbell era was about to come to a close as well. The Eagles were not a winning team under the Swamp Fox, but at least they had their sights set on reaching the .500 mark after playing a very respectable game at San Francisco against a powerful 49ers team with Joe Montana at the controls. The Eagles did not win, but hanging in for 60 minutes in a 23–14 game gave the team some confidence for a week 10 home game against the Falcons.

The Eagles came out fired up and playing very well. With Jaworski at quarterback, they built a 17–0 lead and appeared to be in complete control. But Coach Dan Henning's Falcons—usually an uninspired team—found some life in the fourth quarter. Quarterback David Archer hit scatback Joe Washington with an 18-yard touchdown pass to get Atlanta on the board. The Falcons—who would finish last in the NFC West with a 4–12 record—suddenly came to life and began playing with a purpose. They exerted their will and got themselves back in the game when power runner Gerald Riggs bucked into the end zone from a yard out. Late in the fourth quarter, place-kicker Mick Luckhurst wobbled a 27-yard kick just inside the goal posts to tie the score and send the game into overtime.

Henning thought his team had the Eagles on the run. All that remained was sealing the deal in overtime—the Eagles had nothing left in the tank.

The Falcons had to punt on their first overtime possession, but the kick was downed inside the Philadelphia 1. The Eagles would certainly take the conservative route and try to power the ball out from the goal line to get out of danger. If they could get a first down, great—but the main idea would be to get to at least the 5-yard line so punter Mike Horan would have room to step into his kick and get them out of danger.

At least that's what Henning thought would happen.

Instead, Campbell and the Eagles did something unexpected. On second down, Jaworski took a deep drop in the end zone, hoping to find Quick streaking downfield. Jaworski was not overly confident that the play would work, but he was happy to have the opportunity to take a chance.

Quick ran a post pattern and got by cornerback Bobby Butler, leaving only safety Scott Case to beat. Jaworski thought he had enough arm strength to get the ball to Quick, and he didn't think Case would be able to knock the ball down or find a way to intercept it. He took his shot.

Case saw the ball leave Jaworski's hand and he thought he could get to it. He went for the interception, but he wasn't quick

Getty Images

Mike Quick's catch of a short Ron Jaworski pass, and subsequent 99-yard dash to the end zone, led to a 1985 overtime victory against the Falcons. It shines as one of the great plays in Philly football history.

enough; instead, it hit the streaking Quick between the numbers. Once he caught it, all he had to do was keep running into the end zone for a shocking 99-yard touchdown.

Quick was surprised to hear Jaworski make the call that set the play in motion, but he was glad the team had decided not to go the conservative route. It was clear to Quick that the Falcons were focusing on hemming the Eagles in by stopping the run. He knew that he would still face double coverage, but he thought that he might be able to beat Case because the safety would be guessing on

THE PUNT

Randall Cunningham holds the record for the longest punt in Eagles history. He stood deep in his own end zone in a 1989 game against the Giants in the Meadowlands with the score tied 17–17 in the fourth quarter. The winds were gusting mightily but that did not bother Cunningham. He waited calmly for the snap and booted a 91-yarder.

The ball was driven high and deep in the air and flew 70 yards in the air and touched ground at the Giants 38-yard line. After it hit the ground, the ball bounced by Giants return specialist Dave Meggett and didn't stop until it reached the Giants 16.

Philadelphia Inquirer writer Jay Searcy said the punt was "so high and long that it must have traveled through heaven."

The punt also changed the game as the Eagles defense was completely fired up when it took the field. Eagles defensive tackle Mike Golic forced a Phil Simms fumble—one of the big guy's rare sacks—and Mike Pitts recovered. Keith Byars took advantage by ramming the ball into the end zone three plays later for a 24–17 win.

Cunningham had been a big-time punter during his college career at UNLV, but that skill was rarely put into play once he reached the NFL. However, Cunningham always practiced his punting and special teams coach Al Roberts knew that Cunningham had a huge leg. Eagles punter Max Runager was quite consistent, but he lacked the huge leg. So he understood why the Eagles went with Cunningham at that point in the game since they needed power and not direction.

Cunningham called the kick "the best one of his life," whether it had been in a game, practice, or in the schoolyard. It also led the Eagles to a key victory that helped them make the playoffs as a wild card qualifier.

the run and would not be inclined to backpedal.

"I knew I could get them on that play," Quick explained. "The key was finding a way to beat Butler, because Butler was not going to catch me if he wasn't able to slow me down. I got a clean release, Jaws put the ball in there, and I had an open field. The only thing that would stop me was if I tripped and fell."

There would be none of that. True to form, Quick picked up the pace after he caught the ball and streaked into the end zone to earn the win for the Eagles and get the team to the .500 mark.

Having completely misdiagnosed the Eagles' mind-set, Henning was able to appreciate the execution of the play that had killed his team's chances. "We got beaten by a great athlete [Quick] making a great play," Henning said. "You hate to lose, but at least it was on a sensational play. If we have to get beat, that's the way I want it to happen—on a sensational play."

"I'll never forget that play," Jaworski said. "We had lost a 17–0 lead and there was not a great feeling on the sideline. I'm not saying we stopped believing, but confidence was not incredibly high.

"But as soon as we got to the line, I saw that we had a good chance to be successful based on the way they lined up. Once he [Quick] beat Butler, I decided I was going to take a shot. The safety must not have thought I had much arm strength left [Jaworski was 34 at the time], but I surprised him, because the ball had some zip on it."

There's another reason why Jaworski will never forget this particular play: Steve Sabol, one of the founders of NFL Films and the organization's current president, has made the play one of their signature clips through the years.

Did reaching the .500 mark at 5–5 propel the Eagles to a new level? Hardly. While they won the following week against the Cardinals in St. Louis, Philadelphia dropped four of its last five games to finish in fourth place, ending its fourth straight season without reaching the playoffs.

CHARACTERS IN GREEN

THE UNFORGETTABLE TIM ROSSOVICH

There are few football players who can say that sacrificing their body on the gridiron was among the most sane things they did during their lives. Most have at least some regrets about the physical toll their playing days took on their bodies. Years of abuse often leave players to live out their lives in less than full health.

But don't count former Eagles defensive end and linebacker Tim Rossovich in that group. Not only did "Rossy" throw his body around with reckless abandon on the football field, but he did the same things—and sometimes worse—when he was *not* playing.

Rossovich was known for his strange behavior, long hair, and violating the team's draconian dress code. At a time when all players were required to keep their hair short and to follow the rules to the letter, Rossovich developed his own style. He had long, curly hair that looked something like an Afro and wore bold and colorful clothing that startled management and emboldened his fellow players. Johnny Knoxville may be making millions from his *Jackass* television and movie franchise, but he can't hold a candle to the irrepressible Rossovich, who knew no fear on or off the field. He simply refused to let the authorities boss him around when it came to enjoying himself off the field.

"They just didn't understand the changes from the decades before," Rossovich told author Fran Zimunich in his book *Where Have They Gone?* "It was the 1960s and people had long hair and facial hair. I didn't understand why hair codes and dress codes were

Getty Images

Defensive end and linebacker Tim Rossovich gave new meaning to the word colorful with his off-the-field antics and on-field demeanor, but he was also an outstanding football player.

important. They had nothing to do with your performance on the field. I wanted to win. I was very professional toward my job and committed to my teammates. I really cared about the way the game was played and I cared about everybody in the locker room."

There was no doubt that Rossovich was committed to his teammates. But there were also those who would have said that he needed to be committed—to a mental institution. His bizarre behavior included eating glass, setting himself on fire, jumping off a ladder into a whirlpool, and hiding in an ice machine. And all that's just the tip of the iceberg. But his antics had a purpose— he wanted to motivate his teammates to turn the team's fortunes around and win.

The late 1960s and early '70s were a period of rebellion, and the NFL was not immune to such behavior. Rossovich, along with Dallas tight end Pete Gent and Cardinals linebacker Dave Meggyesy, represented the league's most visible rebels. Naturally, the Eagles management and coaching staff were sometimes taken aback by Rossy's actions, but he was a favorite among teammates and fans. He had the kind of unpredictability that kept everyone loose and wondering what he would do next.

Ed Khayat was the coach during Rossovich's career in Philadelphia, and they clashed frequently. Even though Rossovich gave everything he had on every play, his long hair, mustache, and off-the-field antics drove the old-school, Southern-born Khayat up the wall. The coach demanded that his players have short hair and no facial hair, but Rossovich wasn't about to give in to authority.

"It was a different time," Rossovich said. "I wanted people to acknowledge me. Boy, did I get attention. Losing was very distressing, and we worked hard to turn it around. That's what truly motivated me. I wanted to get everybody off their asses and do something to try to win some football games."

The Eagles won all of 15 games during Rossy's four years with the team (1968–71), but he nonetheless left an indelible imprint on the city. Philadelphia left an equally huge impression on Rossovich, a West Coast boy from the University of Southern California who happened to room with future TV star Tom Selleck during his days as a Trojan.

"I honestly knew nothing of the East Coast," Rossovich said. "I didn't know what to expect, but I was happy and proud to have been drafted in the first round. It was just great to be considered among the first rounders, let alone actually picked that high. I also liked the challenge of it. I knew I had some talent and I had worked hard to develop my skills. It was an opportunity to show what I could do against the best."

Rossovich soon found out that Eagles fans were more passionate about their team than perhaps any other group in the country. "Philly is probably both the best and worst town to play football," Rossovich said. "The fans are behind you 1,000 percent until you make a mistake. They are the most aggressive fans in the country.

I have wonderful memories of them. Like the time I went to the Spectrum [an indoor arena] for a Rolling Stones concert. They called me up [on stage] and I got more screams than Mick Jagger. It's a blue-collar town with honest people. Interacting with the people there was my best experience."

Rossovich went on to play for the Chargers, the Oilers, and the World Football League's Philadelphia Bell. Once his football career was over he did not choose to shun the spotlight. He became an actor and stuntman in the years that followed, appearing in movies such as *The Sting II, The Long Riders*, and *The Main Event*. He also appeared on television in *Mike Hammer, Private Eye; Baywatch; Magnum, P.I.* (alongside former roommate Selleck); and *MacGyver*.

Rossovich has basically retired to the good life in Grass Valley, California, but he'd likely jump right back into the spotlight if the right part or stunt came along—the more challenging, the better.

What else would you expect from a player who used to light his hair on fire for fun?

THE TERRELL OWENS SAGA

Terrell Owens is among the most controversial athletes ever to play pro sports. Undeniably talented, with tremendous physical tools, Owens also has a nonstop ego that has caused problems for him at every stop in his career.

Controversy is no stranger to Philadelphia. This is the city where Dick (then Richie) Allen traced the word *Boo* in the dirt at first base with his baseball spikes because that's how he was regularly greeted by Phillies fans. Allen Iverson, who played much of his career with the Philadelphia 76ers, is perhaps the most competitive basketball player of his generation, but his image of unpredictability and danger mixed with outspoken immaturity ultimately made him a liability.

Owens would turn out to be both a savior and a wrecking ball for the Eagles. Unhappy with his salary and the "lack of respect" shown him by the San Francisco 49ers, Owens engineered a three-way trade between the Niners, the Eagles, and the Baltimore

Terrell Owens addresses the media outside his Moorestown, New Jersey, home in August 2005. Eagles coach Andy Reid ejected Owens from training camp, adding that the tempestuous wide receiver would not be permitted back to camp until the two of them had a chance to sit down and discuss Owens's problem.

Ravens that saw him end up in an Eagles uniform after signing a seven-year, $49 million contract. But the contract—signed against the advice of the players union—ultimately led to a perfect storm of ill will between the Eagles and Owens (egged on by his controversial agent, Drew Rosenhaus).

But let's not get ahead of ourselves. The Eagles went after

Owens prior to the 2004 season because they had a terrible hole at the wide receiver position. Head coach Andy Reid had taken his team to three straight NFC Championship games—against the Rams, Bucs, and Panthers—and had lost all three. A weakness at the wideout position factored greatly in all of those defeats.

The fans were demanding new blood and an upgrade in talent. Owens, the focus of those demands, was a brute of a wide receiver with a flair for self-promotion. He was a well-known star in 2002, but that season he exploded into the public eye when he scored a touchdown against the Seattle Seahawks in a Monday night game. After the play he pulled a "Sharpie" marker out of his sock to autograph the football, which he then presented to his financial adviser.

The Eagles may not have been interested in the sideshow, but they did want to get their hands on a 6'4", 220-pound star who changed games with his ability to go downfield and make the big play. Owens had a hunger to perform in the spotlight, while Reid had dreams of teaming him with Donovan McNabb to get the Eagles over the hump.

In 2004 Owens proved to be just the receiver the Eagles had been looking for. He started his tenure in Philadelphia with a bang, catching eight passes for 64 yards and three touchdowns in a 31–17 Philadelphia win against the New York Giants. Not only was he a dominating performer, he was an exuberant one as well, and all eyes in the stands at Lincoln Financial Field were on him at all times.

Owens would go on to score 14 touchdowns, building what seemed to be a first-rate partnership with McNabb. If the Eagles continued to win, they would gain home-field advantage in the NFC title game once again—and surely, with Owens now on their side, this time they would get over the top to take the long-suffering Eagles back to the Super Bowl for the first time since Dick Vermeil led the 1980 Birds to a disastrous date with the Raiders.

Owens was both consistent and spectacular. He scored touchdowns in all but three of the team's first 12 games and added another three touchdown performances in the team's first meeting of the season with Dallas.

Owens also showed that his change in uniform had done nothing to harm his creativity. Known for his "routines" after scoring touchdowns, Owens would often pantomime a bird in flight to signal his kinship with the Eagles and their fans. In a week eight home game with the Ravens, Owens mockingly gyrated his hips after scoring a touchdown. The action was meant to disrespect Baltimore Raven middle linebacker Ray Lewis, who had disparaged Owens when the receiver balked at the idea of playing for Baltimore.

Yet despite Owens's great statistics—and his arrogant, if entertaining, shenanigans—all was not well. Owens made no attempt to hide his dissatisfaction whenever he was not the center of attention. If McNabb made a poor throw or—gasp!—threw the ball to another receiver, Owens wouldn't hesitate to let McNabb know what he thought about it. This might have been acceptable if he had taken up his disagreements with the quarterback behind closed doors in the locker room, but that was not going to happen with Owens. He openly called McNabb out on the sideline, demanding the football. McNabb, a reasonable man, probably would have listened to Owens had he presented his point of view in a mature fashion. But Owens chose to act like an immature peacock, pointing his finger at the quarterback and preening for the cameras.

It was an uncomfortable marriage, but it still somehow managed to produce. It also provided great promise for the post-season. But those plans went up in smoke when Owens fractured his fibula in a week 15 game against the Cowboys. Publicly, the Eagles claimed there was a chance that Owens could back in the game in time for the Super Bowl (if they got that far), but few believed that kind of injury could heal that fast.

Owens, however, never wavered. This was his first chance to play in a Super Bowl, and if he had to do the impossible to get into the game, he would do it. His desire to play seemed admirable, but many questioned his motives. During the season, he had hired the confrontational Rosenhaus as his new representation. The first thing Rosenhaus told Owens was that the contract he had signed was substandard and that they would be able to secure Owens a new contract at much better terms in the off-season. But to best promote his client and make his case before the public, Rosenhaus would need Owens to pull off a big performance in the Super Bowl. Owens's broken leg was a huge obstacle that he would need to overcome if he was going to get his "respect"—and his cash.

During the week prior to the Super Bowl meeting with the Patriots in Jacksonville, Reid kept his mind open to the possibility of an Owens recovery, but he did not really believe it would happen. Owens meanwhile insisted he would be fine to play, even if it meant going against the advice of the surgeon who had repaired his leg.

Owens did play—and brilliantly—in the big game, catching nine passes against the vicious New England defense for 122 yards. But the Patriots still outlasted the Eagles, winning 24–21, and the way the game ended raised some eyebrows in the Philadelphia locker room.

Trailing 24–14 with 5:40 remaining in the fourth quarter, McNabb and the Eagles took possession at their own 21. Needing two scores, everyone expected the Eagles to go into a hurry-up, no-huddle offense. But that did not happen; instead, they used 12 plays to nickel-and-dime their way down the field, gaining 49 yards. They huddled before every play, and there appeared to be a strange lack of urgency. The Eagles finally scored when McNabb hit tight end Greg Lewis with a 30-yard touchdown pass, but at that point there was only 1:48 left on the clock.

Philadelphia went for an onside kick, and the Pats recovered it. After the Eagles called a timeout following three consecutive running plays by the Pats, the Eagles got the ball back at their own 4-yard line with only 46 seconds remaining. With Eagles fans praying for a miracle, McNabb instead threw an interception. The Patriots had their third Super Bowl title in four years.

The slow play in the game's final moments was a big item in the postgame press coverage, and Reid answered questions about it cryptically. "We were trying to hurry up," he said. It made no sense. Something stunk badly on the west side of Jacksonville.

In the days that followed, Eagles players told the media that

McNabb had a difficult time catching his breath at the end of the game, which was played in relatively high humidity—at least compared to the norm in Philadelphia—and that he was unable to go any faster. Wideout Freddie "Hollywood" Mitchell claimed McNabb was so sick that he was about to "puke" during the drive.

McNabb and Reid denied those charges, but they surfaced again later in the off-season when Owens was looking for publicity as he attempted to reopen contract negotiations with the Eagles. Owens didn't mention McNabb's name when he was asked about what happened at the end of the Super Bowl, but it was obvious that he was throwing his quarterback under the bus. "Why are you asking me?" he said. "I wasn't the one who got tired in the Super Bowl."

That was the beginning of the end for Owens in Philadelphia. Instead of treating his quarterback as an ally, he had publicly skewered him. McNabb had nothing but contempt for Owens after that and wasn't about to take his side in any contract squabble.

As the off-season went on, Owens and Rosenhaus continued to make new demands on the Eagles in an attempt to renegotiate a deal that the receiver had signed just a year earlier. Reid and owner Jeff Lurie, on the other hand, were not about to be bullied despite the fact that they had no leverage at the wideout position.

The situation appeared to have the potential to get ugly, but nobody could have known just what depths it would eventually reach.

THE ONE-MAN WRECKING CREW

It was all downhill for Owens after his thrilling comeback performance in the Super Bowl. Instead of taking advantage of his great game and turning himself into a core member of the Eagles, he instead decided to turn himself into a sideshow clown while grabbing for all the money he could get.

Rosenhaus fed Owens's outsized ego and promised that he would find a way to get Owens a better deal. Rosenhaus certainly had calm waters to negotiate following the brilliant Super Bowl showing, but every move made by the receiver and his agent ended up turning public sentiment against them.

Trashing McNabb was the first of many mistakes. The comment angered Eagles fans and management, and it also turned a powerful ally into an enemy. Many in the organization had thought that McNabb and Owens could form a great partnership, like Peyton Manning and Marvin Harrison in Indianapolis or Carson Palmer and Chad Johnson in Cincinnati. But it soon became obvious that that goal would never come to fruition. It was clear that Owens had little time for McNabb, whom he almost never looked at or talked to on the sideline.

Most rational football fans and media had no idea what Owens was thinking. It had never been likely that Eagles management would change Owens's contract to begin with, but his spoiled, churlish behavior ensured that Lurie would tell him to stay out of his office. The Eagles did not want to set a bad precedent by reopening the deal and coddling Owens like a spoiled child.

Owens dug in and decided to put on a memorable show—one that would ruin his reputation in Philadelphia and the rest of the thinking world. He didn't go to minicamp. He complained about the way he was being treated in public. He said that he was not looking to take advantage of anyone or anything, but that he "just wanted to be able to feed his family." Nobody was more appreciative of those remarks than late night talk-show hosts David Letterman and Jay Leno, who both had a field day at Owens's expense. By the time training camp was about to start, Owens was clearly a major distraction. He regularly questioned the team in public. Everyone wanted to know if he would show up at the Eagles' training facility at Lehigh University—and if he did, how would he behave?

Quite badly, as it turned out.

Tiring of the Owens circus, head coach Reid booted Owens from camp and suspended him for a week. Once Owens got back to his home in Moorestown, New Jersey, he was not about to learn his lesson and start behaving. The media and crowds of civilians descended on his home, and nobody loved it more than the attention-hungry T.O. He decided to put on a memorable show. The muscular receiver brought a weight bench out to his driveway, stripped to the waist to show off his physique, and did a few crunches for all who cared to take photos or observe.

Any shred of dignity that Owens had previously owned flew out the window. He was digging his own grave in Philadelphia and using heavy equipment to do it. How could any self-respecting Eagles fan or observer support him or his buffoonish behavior? Owens not only wanted more money, he was also humiliating the team's management, coaches, players, and fans with his actions. His public support had simply evaporated.

Owens lost any shred of support he might have had left on October 9, when the Eagles dropped a 33–10 game to the Cowboys in Dallas. After the game, Owens was seen wearing a Dallas throwback jersey with a No. 88 on the back and Hall of Fame wide receiver Michael Irvin's name on it. When pictures of Owens in Dallas garb reached Eagles fans, they were livid with the receiver and angry with Reid for putting up with him. Reid decided to let Owens have it, and the Eagles suspended him for four games on November 5.

Unfortunately, the suspension did nothing to quiet Owens. He filed a grievance against the team, but the hearing only made him look worse. Testimony from coaches and team management revealed Owens's history of childish behavior and selfishness—including parking in handicapped spaces at Lincoln Financial Field.

In addition to Owens's distractions, the team suffered many injuries that season. The low point came when they absorbed a 42–0 home defeat to Seattle during a week 13 Monday night game. The team released Owens shortly after the regular season ended. He had torn the team apart and would never be welcome again in a Philadelphia uniform. The toxic legacy he left behind had painful ramifications as the Eagles struggled to rebuild a depleted receiver corps.

Cowboys owner Jerry Jones, wanting to upgrade at the wide receiver position, was tempted to bring Owens to Dallas. Jones knew head coach Bill Parcells would not be thrilled with the idea, but he decided to go for it anyway. Owens endured a number of nagging and serious injuries during the 2006 season, and it was clear that he was still the same whiny, difficult player he had been in San Francisco and Philadelphia. When he claimed that a hamstring injury kept him from practicing in training camp, Parcells's resentment was palpable. He verbalized his disgust for Owens by referring to him only as *the player* or *him,* rather than by name.

Owens further weaseled his way into the public consciousness with a supposed suicide attempt on September 26, 2006. He later said that the incident was just a misunderstanding. His publicist, Kim Etheredge, said that Owens had accidentally taken a combination of pain pills and supplements. But she then threw oil on the fire by saying, "He wouldn't consider such a thing. He has $25 million reasons to live."

Etheredge's ignorant remarks succeeded in taking the spotlight off Owens for a moment as prominent members of the mental health services community disparaged her statement throughout the media. Did Etheredge really think that people with money never suffered from emotional or mental problems?

Owens complained throughout his first season; back in Philly, Reid could only smile as he watched Parcells grow tired of trying to coach this immature baby in a Superman's body. Although the Cowboys did manage to limp into the playoffs as a wild-card team, Parcells decided he could take no more and retired at the end of the season. The Cowboys told anyone who would listen that Owens had nothing to do with Parcells's decision—but nobody believed it, and the NFL is poorer because of Parcells's departure. Despite his curmudgeonly image, Parcells is a great coach who brings a fascinating unpredictability to professional football. But Owens's behavior made Parcells sick, and he decided he just couldn't take it any more.

That's the T.O. effect in a nutshell.

OWENS TIMELINE

Courtesy of *The Philadelphia Inquirer*

2000—During a September contest in Dallas, Owens celebrated scoring a touchdown for the 49ers by running to midfield at Texas Stadium and posing on the Cowboys' star logo. He later repeated his actions following another touchdown but was then blindsided by the Cowboys' George Teague.

2001—After the 49ers blew a 19-point lead in Chicago and lost in overtime, the disgruntled receiver accused San Francisco head coach Steve Mariucci of protecting good friend Dick Jauron, head coach of the Bears.

2002—In an October Monday Night Football game in Seattle, Owens pulled a Sharpie marker out of his sock after catching a touchdown pass for the 49ers. He then proceeded to autograph the ball and hand it to his financial adviser, who was sitting in an end zone luxury suite rented by Shawn Springs, the Seahawks cornerback he had just beaten on the play.

2002—After scoring a touchdown in a December contest with the Green Bay Packers, Owens celebrated with a pair of pom-poms borrowed from a 49ers cheerleader.

2003—Following a bumpy season that included several sideline tirades from Owens, he and the 49ers decided to part ways.

2004—Owens's agent failed to meet a free-agency deadline in March, making him ineligible to become a free agent. Because they still retained his rights, the 49ers then traded him to the Baltimore Ravens, but Owens refused to report to his new team. He expressed a desire to play in Philadelphia and filed a grievance, claiming he should be granted free agency. After a series of negotiations, a deal was worked out between the three teams that sent Owens to Philadelphia, where he signed a seven-year, $49-million deal—against the advice of the players union.

2004—In an interview with *Playboy* magazine, Owens hinted that ex-teammate Jeff Garcia was gay, a claim he later recanted.

2004—After scoring a touchdown in an October contest with the Baltimore Ravens, Owens openly mocked Ray Lewis by performing the middle linebacker's trademark celebration dance.

2004—In a Monday night contest the following month, Owens appeared in a controversial skit to kick off the network's presentation of the game; the skit resulted in an FCC investigation.

2005—Owens hired agent Drew Rosenhaus in April and then announced that he was not happy with his contract. He also told CNBC that, despite making $7.5 million in 2004, he needed a new contract to "feed his family."

2005—After hinting that he might not report to training camp, Owens showed up with a bad attitude, refusing to acknowledge the media or speak to his teammates. After a confrontation with head coach Reid, he was suspended for a week.

2005—During an interview with ESPN's Graham Bensinger on November 3, Owens took shots at the Eagles franchise for not publicly recognizing his 100th touchdown catch, saying that the Eagles showed a "lack of class." He also suggested that the Eagles would be better off with Packers quarterback Brett Favre instead of Donovan McNabb. On November 4 he issued a halfhearted apology through the media for his statements, but failed to deliver comments regarding McNabb, something that head coach Reid had insisted that he include. He was then suspended for the club's contest against the Washington Redskins on November 6. On November 7 Owens's suspension was stretched to four games, and Reid added that Owens would not play for the remainder of the season.

2006—On March 14 the Eagles cut Owens just one day before he was due to receive a $5 million roster bonus.

2006—On July 5 Owens released a tell-all book revealing his side of the story associated with his time in Philadelphia. Then on July 13 he claimed he was misquoted in his own autobiography. Owens blamed his coauthor for using the word heroic to describe his return for Super Bowl XXXIX.

2006—On August 3 Owens missed the first of 14 consecutive days of practice for the Cowboys because of a hamstring problem—but an MRI two days later revealed no major problems. After returning to practice for several days, Owens claimed to have re-aggravated the injury because his coaches pushed him back to the playing field too soon. This time he didn't return to practice until August 29.

2006—On August 10, while still out with an injured hamstring, Owens drew attention to himself by wearing the silver and blue uniform of Lance Armstrong's Discovery Channel pro cycling team while riding a stationary bicycle on the sideline.

2006—On September 26 Owens was taken by ambulance to Baylor University Medical Center due to what was thought to be a suicide attempt. The following day he denied trying to kill himself, claiming that a mixture of pain pills and supplements had caused him to be "out of it" when talking to emergency respondents.

2006—On October 11 Owens had a run-in with Dallas receivers coach Todd Haley. After T.O. was chastised for showing up late for practice (he later claimed that he had been in the bathroom), Owens and Haley tangled during a meeting later in the day.

2006—In a victory over the Atlanta Falcons on December 16 Owens spit in the face of cornerback DeAngelo Hall.

THE INDOMITABLE VINCE PAPALE

Vince Papale was brought back to the public's attention when the movie *Invincible* was released in 2006, but many Philadelphia fans had never forgotten his inspiring story. In addition to chronicling Papale's incredible rise, the movie does an outstanding job of showing how much the Eagles mean to the city of Philadelphia.

Papale, a South Philadelphia school teacher who was struggling to find his way in life, first came to the Eagles' attention when rookie head coach Vermeil held open tryouts in 1976 at Veterans Stadium prior to the start of training camp. Papale's wife had recently left him, leaving behind a painful good-bye note stating that he would never have any money and wouldn't be anything but a disappointment. Papale kept that note and used it as inspiration as he tried to prove his ex-wife wrong.

In the movie, the tryouts were characterized as having all the organization of a three-ring circus, with athletes of all shapes and sizes showing up to try to live the dream of playing professional football. In reality the event was quite organized. Vermeil wanted it to serve two purposes. First, it would reconnect the team—which had suffered badly since winning its last championship in 1960—with the city that had suffered along with them. Eagles fans had never stopped loving their team, but its history of

Vince Papale, the inspiration for Walt Disney Pictures' movie *Invincible*, chats during a press interview in Philadelphia in August 2006.

failure had robbed them of any legitimate reason for optimism. Vermeil also wanted to send a message to the players he had inherited. He felt that the Eagles on the roster at that time had neither the talent nor the commitment to become a winning NFL team. He hoped to turn things around any way he could, and letting his players know that the team might be able to find more competent players through tryouts was effective.

In reality Vermeil and his staff were not expecting to find any worthwhile players at the tryouts. By the mid-1970s the NFL scouting process had grown to the point that any player of decent ability would be found. A talented player from a Division II or Division III school who lacked size and strength might occasionally slip through the process, but the idea of finding a legitimate talent off the street was ludicrous.

But nobody told that to Papale, a first-rate athlete who nearly made the U.S. Olympic team as a decathlete in 1976. Papale knew the odds of making the team were slim, but he also knew that he could run well, and he was going to seize this opportunity to prove himself.

His 4.5 time in the 40-yard dash opened the coaches' eyes, and Papale was pulled aside to see if he could also catch passes. He did so quite impressively. Papale had earned his shot.

"I don't know that he [Vermeil] was really expecting to find anything at those tryouts, but he told me I would get a fair chance at training camp," Papale said. "He was as good as his word, and I had my shot."

For Papale, the experience had a bit of a déjà vu feeling about it. In 1974 Gary Davidson started the World Football League (WFL), a new organization that hoped to compete with the NFL. The WFL decided that summer football was the best way to do it. The WFL held open tryouts—just as Vermeil would two years later—and Papale showed up and won a starting spot for the Philadelphia Bell. Unfortunately for Papale, the WFL was unable to sustain itself after an initial blush of success, and the league soon folded.

The odds against Papale winning a spot with the Eagles were extraordinary. He was a 30-year-old free agent with limited expe-

TIMMY BROWN

The Eagles colors may be green and white, but they probably could have borrowed one of their slogans from UPS.

"Let Brown do it."

Bob "Boomer" Brown was perhaps the best offensive tackle of his era. Jerome Brown was an outstanding defensive tackle who may have been even more valuable in the locker room.

The Brown who often gets overlooked was star running back Timmy Brown. He played in the NFL from 1959 through 1968 and was with the Eagles from 1960–1967. Brown was a great athlete who was drafted by the Green Bay Packers and the NBA's Philadelphia Warriors. He was cut by the Packers after a season and did little with the Eagles in his first two years. But he got an opportunity to show what he could do in 1964 and he set an NFL record with 2,425 combined yards (rushing, receiving, and return).

At that point he became one of the most dangerous threats in the league. Brown always believed in himself but he just didn't have the opportunity to get his hands on the football with much frequency early in his career.

Brown was a small player—5' 11" and 195 pounds—from Ball State University. He didn't have an impressive pedigree and many of his older teammates didn't think he was special. But he became a fan favorite because of his explosive speed and friendly attitude.

Brown was traded to the Baltimore Colts in 1968 and his career lasted just one more season.

Brown was more than just an athlete. After his playing career was over, he went on to become an actor. Brown is best known for his roles in *MASH* (the TV series and the movie) and *Nashville* (the Robert Altman movie), but he was also appeared in a number of television series, including *Mission: Impossible, Cannon, T.J. Hooker, Remington Steele,* and *Gimme a Break.*

But a generation of football fans will remember him as the Eagles' top offensive threat in an era when they didn't have many.

BURK'S BIG DAY

Joe Montana never did it. Neither did Johnny Unitas, Dan Marino, or Brett Favre for that matter.

However, a quick check of the NFL record book shows that Adrian Burk is listed right next to Sid Luckman of the Bears, George Blanda of the Houston Oilers, Y.A. Tittle of the Giants, and Joe Kapp of the Vikings as the quarterbacks who have thrown seven touchdown passes in a single game.

Just who is Adrian Burk? He was a quarterback for the Eagles from 1951 through 1956 and also played one year with the Baltimore Colts. Burk was actually a decent NFL player who made the Pro Bowl in 1954 and 1955.

However, his October 17, 1954, performance against the Washington Redskins in Griffith Stadium was completely off the chart. He threw seven touchdown passes in the Eagles 49–21 victory. Burk did not have a huge passing day—he was 19-of-27 for 229 yards—but the Eagles used the passing game whenever they were around the Washington goal line.

If it hadn't been for Eagles publicity director Ed Hogan, Burk would not have had a chance to tie Luckman's record that had been set in 1943. Burk had thrown six touchdown passes and head coach Jim Trimble had taken Burk out of the game. When Hogan informed Trimble that Burk had a chance to tie the record for most touchdown passes in a game, the coach sent him back on the field and he made the most of his opportunity by throwing his seventh TD pass of the day, to Hall of Famer Pete Pihos, who finished the day with three scoring catches.

After his playing career, Burk went on to become an NFL official. Ironically, he was working the game in 1969 in which Kapp put his name in the record book with his own seven-touchdown performance against the Baltimore Colts.

rience playing organized football. He was a hard-nosed guy from South Philly who played football in the street, but that was about it. But what he lacked in experience, Papale made up for in toughness, heart, and enthusiasm. He also had the benefit of excellent athleticism, as evidenced by his time in the 40 and his competitiveness on the field.

Every time Vermeil was faced with a cutdown date during the

1976 training camp, Papale's name was brought up. But there was something about his heart and personality that came across to Vermeil when he observed Papale on the field. It was not just his hard-luck, neighborhood guy story. Papale played with a level of determination that was impossible to ignore. Vermeil could see that Papale had an interesting combination of speed, strength, and intangibles that might just help the team improve.

"Vince showed us talent," Vermeil explained. "What you're looking for is a real sleeper, or a guy who can come in and make a contribution—even if it's only at training camp—with talent and an attitude that can get the players around him hungry and ready to play. Vince displayed great passion and the desire for an opportunity that he then made the very best of. As for his skill set, once he was given a chance to show it, he was athletic enough to be a wide receiver, but where he really excelled was as a fine punt-return and kickoff defender." Vermeil had been the NFL's first special teams coach, taking a position with the Los Angeles Rams in 1969. Known for his tearful speeches to his players and his equally weepy press conferences, Vermeil was not afraid to follow his emotions when evaluating football talent. He had a gift for finding undrafted players who could actually contribute. Papale was not the only such player to be given a shot by Vermeil; Herman Edwards was an undrafted free agent who went on to a brilliant playing and coaching career after Vermeil found him, and Kurt Warner was bagging groceries when Vermeil gave him a chance to try out for the St. Louis Rams. He eventually led that team to the Super Bowl title following the 1999 season.

Papale went on to play for three seasons with the Eagles; his career ended after he spent the 1979 season on the injured reserve list. But Papale had his NFL highlights, one of which the movie underscored in its climax. After a winless preseason and a punishing 27–7 loss at Dallas in the opener, the pressure was on Vermeil to get a win in the home opener against a New York Giants team that appeared to have little chance to succeed in 1976. The Eagles came up with a big effort that earned them a 20–7 victory. The highlight of the game was a special-teams play by Papale. After racing downfield in punt coverage, Papale made the big hit and forced a fumble that he then recovered in Giants territory to set up a touchdown. It was exactly the kind of play that marked Papale's fearless and inspirational career with the Eagles.

Papale and his story had an influence on the 2006 Eagles, who rebounded from a 6–10 season in 2005 to earn a 10–6 record and first-place in the NFC East. Prior to the week 16 game at Dallas, head coach Reid played the movie for the team in an effort to get his players fired up. The Eagles won the game 23–7 and went on to take the division title with a 10–6 record.

In an interview with IGN Sports, Papale spoke about the movie *Invincible* **and his career.**

IGN Sports: The note your ex-wife wrote you was cold-blooded.

Papale: It was what it was. Maybe it wasn't so cold-blooded. Maybe I needed a wake-up call. I didn't think I did, but whatever it was, it certainly was a motivating factor along with a few other things that were going on in my life. What wasn't shown in the movie is that I was denied an opportunity to tryout for the Olympic decathlon in '72 when I had qualified for them. So that was pretty cold-blooded as well, because I didn't have the right pedigree. Those were the two big motivating factors.

IGN Sports: Why didn't anything about your track background make it into the movie? I was wondering how a 30-year-old was out there running a 4.5 40.

Papale: That's maybe one thing that they might have wanted to touch at, and I know it was considered, but I knew I was going to be out on a speaking tour and I could set the record straight.

IGN Sports: The scenes of the street football game were brutal. Was it that bad in real life?

Papale: It was like that, yeah. Two of the missing things in the movie, though, were the cops and the ambulance. They were always there as key ingredients. They [the filmmakers] took a little liberty, of course, with me playing a street game the week I would be playing an NFL game, but where they got that from was when I was playing in the World Football

League, I was playing Rough Touch in between my games. So they tied that one in. But the themes, and the roughness of the play, they were nothing compared to how they were in real life. We got to the point where we really did need to have police on board all the time. You know the game is rough when cops and an ambulance are a requirement.

IGN Sports: So after getting slammed into cars, playing special teams in the NFL is nothing.

Papale: I said that one time and people started riding me. I said that after playing in the Rough Touch bar leagues, the hits in the NFL are nothing. They don't even compare. I took some good-natured ribbing from my teammates about that article, but it was true. And it certainly prepared me for training camp and for the free-agent tryout where I did run that 4.5 40. Guys at that tryout were trying to take my head off because there was a lot of one-on-one stuff going on and guys were trying to rip me apart, but I kept thinking if I could survive the Rough Touch leagues, I could survive anything.

IGN Sports: What was the tryout really like? The movie made it look like a circus.

Papale: It wasn't a circus. That was a little bit of Hollywood, but it played really well. But there were a lot of guys out there who were absolutely sincere and serious despite their condition, especially the green cape guy. He's actually an actor and a steakhouse owner in Philadelphia—his name is Tony Luke Jr.—and these guys were absolutely convinced that they would be better than what they saw out on the field. I just wanted to get a shot, and it's a "speed kills" theory. Coach Vermeil saw how fast I could run, and the next thing is, can I catch the ball, so they threw a few at me. It all just fell into place from there. I was offered my big first contract in the NFL. I was offered $21,000 to play back then. Twenty-one thousand dollars, baby. Actually, back then, it wasn't bad money.

IGN Sports: Unfortunately, you missed the Super Bowl against the Raiders.

Papale: Yeah, I was injured and that was it. I had a dislocated left shoulder and a separated right shoulder. I got my four years in. I spent my fourth year on injured reserve, but my fifth year, the team had some younger receivers who needed to get a shot. I didn't get a shot to be on that Super Bowl team, and it was tough at first, I had a tough time with it because I swore I could've been a positive factor, a contributing factor in it. But I got four years out of it, I got a great opportunity by Dick Vermeil, so I'm not going to be greedy.

IGN Sports: In your eyes, what makes Coach Vermeil unique among the NFL elite?

Papale: One thing about him is he cares. He gets to know his players. He gets to know them for more than what they are as football players. He gets to know them off the field. He gets to know their families. The relationship between Dick Vermeil and my father was extraordinary. He just respected my father so much, it was cool. And Dick, just like every coach who is successful, one of the things we liked was his enthusiasm and his passion. And he has that passion for everything, not just football. Dick is a man's man, a renaissance man. He's a mechanic, a great cook, he's a wine guy, a hunter, and he's just a nice, genuine, honest guy. I think that's what separates him from the rest of the people. Not that others aren't honest, but Dick is just so straightforward, he's a beautiful person. He's the type of guy you can trust.

IGN Sports: But he never cried in the movie.

Papale: Because he wasn't a crier that first year. I don't ever remember him shedding a tear that first year. His second year, as we started to turn things around, his emotions would get a hold of him every once in a while, but that first year, the closest he got were tears of anger or pain from clenching his teeth so much, but never tears of emotion. But I'll tell you, that second year, especially after the Miracle in the Meadowlands, and when he knew we were going to make the playoffs, he just let all of his Italian out.

IGN Sports: Since you were a longtime Eagles season ticket holder, were you part of the crowd that booed Santa Claus?

Papale: I was in that crowd, but I didn't boo Santa Claus. But keep in mind, that was not the Santa Claus that was supposed to be out there. That was the Santa Claus that came out of the stands that was stone drunk, and he thought he was going to play the part. They just picked somebody because the real Santa Claus who was supposed to show up never showed, so the organizers of the event saw some guy dressed as Santa and they put him on the field. He was stumbling all over himself and he looked like a commercial for a bad disease for losing weight. The fans of Philadelphia rode him hard, but the fans of Philadelphia got a bum rap for it because it wasn't as bad as it seemed. That's how it actually happened, and I guess we'll just have to take that rap for the rest of our lives. It's even in the movie. [Laughs.] It gets a lot of laughs, but it happened a little differently than people realize.

IGN Sports: These are the same fans, though, that booed Donovan McNabb at the draft.

Papale: Let me tell you about the Philadelphia fans. They're knowledgeable, they're passionate, they're loyal, they spend their money, and they defend their athletes to the max. But at the same time, they're frustrated. They want a winner. We haven't had a winner in a long time. We've gotten so close and we're deserving of one, but we'll see.

IGN Sports: What's your take on heart versus talent in the world of sports? Obviously you can have all the heart in the world with no talent and never make it, but even the most gifted athletes need a little heart to make a difference. What's the percentage of each that would make the perfect athlete?

Papale: In my case, there were guys more talented than me, no doubt about it. I would consider it to be a 70/30 proposition, with talent being 70 and heart being 30. But man, that 30 percent can bring you to 110 percent, and that seems to be what guys are missing right now. I didn't have the pedigree as a football player, but I was a scholarship athlete in track and field, I was an Olympic hopeful, I played basketball and baseball.... There weren't too many sports I couldn't play. I had the talent, but combined with my enthusiasm and passion...that's what drew Dick Vermeil and I together. He liked that other side of me. The fact that I was a school-teacher, he was a schoolteacher. The fact that my father was a mechanic, his father was a mechanic. There were a lot of things that paralleled our lives, and I think he took all of those things into consideration when picking me. He went with my heart over talent, and I'll forever be grateful.

UP AND DOWN

THE DONOVAN M^CNABB EXPERIENCE

It started with a torrent of boos on draft day in 1999.

When NFL Commissioner Paul Tagliabue called Donovan McNabb's name as the draft's second pick, Eagles fans in the crowd rained down the sound of their discontent. They did not really have anything against this young, outstanding quarterback who had made a name for himself with his athleticism, arm strength, and versatility at Syracuse University. They were just upset with their team for not drafting Heisman Trophy–winning running back Ricky Williams.

The Eagles had a god-awful running game in 1998, and the fans thought that the multitalented Williams would be just the player they needed. Draftniks had picked apart McNabb in the weeks leading up to the draft, expounding ad nauseam on all his potential weaknesses. Williams, on the other hand, looked like a sure thing to Eagles fans.

So how did Williams work out for the Saints (the team that drafted him) and the Dolphins (the team that traded for him)? The history books tell the tale: not good.

And how about McNabb? He was the second of five quarterbacks taken in the first 12 picks of the 1999 draft. Of the other four, Akili Smith and Cade McNown were absolute busts. Tim Couch, the number one pick, was an abject failure, although to be fair, this was due in large part to injuries. Daunte Culpepper has

Syracuse quarterback Donovan McNabb poses with family and friends after being chosen by the Eagles as the team's first pick, second overall, in the NFL draft in New York in April 1999.

run the gamut from brilliant to awful. McNabb is left as the clear-cut winner among his draft-mates.

But is McNabb a great quarterback?

The answer, sadly, is no. There have been questions about his accuracy as a pocket passer since the start of his career, and injuries have wrecked him in two different seasons. He has been quite good—maybe even very good—at times, but three straight losses by the Eagles in the NFC Championship game (to St. Louis, Tampa Bay, and Carolina), and the team's subsequent failure to bring home the title in the Super Bowl against New England, throw cold water in the faces of those who would like to label him as a great one.

McNabb is a thoughtful and introspective man, and he has never put himself in the same category as the all-time greats of the game. But he has had flashes of greatness throughout his career. In his early years, he excelled at making plays on the run. He threw the ball well on the move and could run with it when he either chose to or needed to do so.

During his first two or three seasons, many opponents tried to challenge McNabb by keeping him in the pocket, preventing him from sprinting out of trouble. That was how defensive coordinators around the league tried to defend against him—until the 2001 divisional playoffs against the Bears.

McNabb, who grew up in Chicago and was a high school legend at Mount Carmel High School before going to Syracuse, was intent on putting on a great show in front of his family and friends. The Eagles had beaten the Tampa Bay Bucs 31–9 in the wild-card game; McNabb had acquitted himself well and won praise from head coach Andy Reid. He came into Chicago loaded with confidence.

The Bears rolled into the playoffs that season with a 13–3 record. Many of their victories had been quite thrilling, including back-to-back overtime wins against San Francisco and Cleveland that had given this team the feeling that destiny was on its side.

But the Bears did not have enough offensive firepower to compete with the Eagles. McNabb ate up their powerful defense, throwing for 262 yards and two touchdowns. He also ran for a touchdown. The Chicago defense had no answer for him.

"McNabb had an excellent game," said the Bears' somnambulant head coach, Dick Jauron. "You have to give him credit for taking what was there and not making mistakes."

Frustration and disappointment were palpable in the Bears locker room, with McNabb's play serving as the focal point for their regrets. "He just killed us," said tackle Blake Brockermeyer. "He got away from us and made plays."

Reid thoroughly enjoyed what he saw from McNabb that day,

believing that it was a seminal moment in the quarterback's development. "I think he showed that he can perform in the biggest games," said Reid. "He took a step forward."

The Eagles came close the following week in the NFC title game against the favored Rams in St. Louis, but ultimately fell short. Still, things definitely seemed to be improving for the Eagles and their up-and-coming quarterback.

In 2002 McNabb fractured his ankle in a game late in the season against the Cardinals. Instead of coming out of the game, he endured the pain and threw four touchdown passes to lead the team to a 38–14 win. By the time he was able to return to the lineup, the Eagles were cruising. They went on to win the NFC East with a 12–4 record.

After beating the Falcons 20–6 in the divisional playoffs, the Eagles were significant favorites against the visiting Bucs, who were coming to Philadelphia for the last game that would ever be played at Veterans Stadium. The Eagles, who had wanted to give their fans something special that day, sadly could not come through; the Bucs shut them down, harassing McNabb into two fumbles. Tampa Bay silenced the Vet in a 27–10 upset; McNabb took the blame when he faced the media.

"I just played poorly," he said. "There were chances to make plays and I didn't make them. This being the last game here at the Vet, we wanted to make it special. That clearly did not happen."

It was déjà vu all over again when the Eagles hosted the Panthers in the NFC title game the following year. Carolina played very aggressively on defense and McNabb threw three interceptions on the way to a 14–3 loss for the Eagles. McNabb took a serious beating; he was sacked four times and was forced out of the game with torn rib cartilage after a second-quarter late hit. He was ineffective once again, and there was a feeling that these three straight losses proved that he just couldn't get past the NFC Championship game.

Earlier that year McNabb had found himself in the middle of a controversy when conservative talk-show host Rush Limbaugh—playing the role of NFL analyst for ESPN—downplayed McNabb's talent, saying that he was overrated by the media because they were "desirous" of seeing a black quarterback do well. Outraged individuals from both the media and the public sector demanded that Limbaugh be dismissed for his comments, which many deemed to be racist. McNabb, however, barely recognized the remarks, saying they were "unfortunate" and noting that the NFL had a number of African Americans playing well at the position. The Eagles went on to win 12 of 14 games after an 0–2 start, playing exceptionally well.

The high-water mark for McNabb came in 2004, when he seemed to be developing a great partnership with big-play wide receiver Terrell Owens; led by T.O. and McNabb, the Eagles dominated the NFC. This time they made it past the NFC Championship game, with a 27–10 win over Atlanta, earning a Super Bowl appearance against New England. But McNabb and the Eagles fell short in that game; they had a chance to come from behind and steal the win, but instead lost 24–21.

After a disastrous 2005 season largely sabotaged by Owens, the Eagles bounced back and were once again a playoff team in 2006. But McNabb, injured for much of the season, was forced to watch journeyman Jeff Garcia take the reins and lead the Eagles down the stretch. There were rumblings in Philadelphia that the Eagles would be better off in the long run if they kept Garcia in the lineup and let the McNabb era come to an end. But Reid was having none of it, and he demonstrated his loyalty to McNabb by releasing Garcia at the end of the season.

As McNabb continues to write the story of his career, his name appears all over the Eagles record book. Is he an all-time great quarterback? Perhaps not. But is he a very good one capable of leading his team in clutch situations? Absolutely. If the Eagles can ever claim that elusive Super Bowl title, McNabb will be remembered for generations as one of the Eagles' all-time greatest players.

JEFF LURIE TO THE RESCUE

Norman Braman did two big favors for Eagles fans.

First, he bought the franchise in 1985 from the distressed Leonard Tose, who had lost so much money to Atlantic City casinos that he considered taking the franchise to Arizona, where

Eagles ownership was upgraded dramatically when Jeffrey Lurie came into the picture.

he had a potential buyer lined up who would purchase part of the team, bringing Tose's finances back into the black while still allowing him to retain control of the team.

But Braman provided Eagles fans with an equally large service when he sold the team to Jeffrey Lurie in 1994. Braman had quickly lost the thrill of owning a franchise, especially when it came to dealing with cantankerous coach Buddy Ryan. While "Buddyball" was a big hit in Philadelphia, his snarling, pugnacious personality was a poor fit with the extremely polished Braman. Ryan liked to refer to Braman as "the guy in France"—and always with a sneer.

Braman, like Tose, made no secret of the fact that he enjoyed the high life, including a private jet and a luxurious residence in the south of France. But when it came to the day-to-day operations of his team, he was a bottom-line guy who took note of every penny that was spent. He was wildly unpopular with players, coaches, and fans alike, and eventually he felt he just didn't need the headache. He decided to cash in his investment by selling to the eager Lurie.

Lurie was a lifelong sports fan born in Boston in 1951. He followed the Bruins, the Celtics, and the Red Sox passionately. He had even attended the first Boston Patriots game, when they were part of the American Football League. He was also quite wealthy, having made tons of money in Hollywood as a film producer in addition to being the heir to the Harcourt General publishing and movie theater businesses.

Naturally a rich and rabid sports fan like Lurie liked the idea of owning his own professional sports franchise; when the Patriots were put up for sale in 1993, he battled Robert Kraft in an attempt to acquire it. But once the price exceeded the $150-million mark, Lurie was forced to drop out of the bidding. He also tried to help Baltimore get an expansion franchise, but he was shot down when the league decided to go with Carolina and Jacksonville.

When he got word that Braman was interested in selling the Eagles, Lurie truly put his heart and soul into the deal. He was the leading candidate throughout the sale process, eventually paying Braman $185 million for the team—an NFL record at the time.

Since that time Lurie and his right-hand man, Joe Banner, have worked with diligence and professionalism to turn the Eagles into one of the steadiest and most dependable franchises in the league. They have been successful both on and off the field. The Eagles went to the playoffs six times between 2000 and 2006, the best stretch in franchise history. While they have not yet won a Super Bowl, they took the NFC title in 2004 and gave the Patriots everything they had in the big game before coming up short.

When he first bought the team it soon became obvious to Lurie that nearly everything about the Eagles was of less than major league quality. The dilapidated conditions in Veterans Stadium shocked him. There were no windows in the team offices, the lighting was terrible, and the same rats that he had seen at the old Boston Garden also held sway in Philadelphia. Morale among Eagles support staff was low.

Lurie set out at once to change the Eagles' second-class status as tenants of less-than-stellar facilities. He immediately decided to build a new stadium and practice facility—one that the franchise would own, rather than having to lease from another sports team or the city. Plans were drawn up for the $512-million Lincoln Financial Field and the 108,000-square-foot team headquarters called the NovaCare Complex.

Lurie has said that his main goal was to change the impression held by NFL administrators and longtime fans that the Eagles simply were not a big-time franchise. "I thought the challenge was to make people see the franchise differently," Lurie said. "We had to start treating ourselves as if we were a state-of-the-art franchise, even if we had quite a ways to go in order to get there."

Lurie also wanted to quell rumors that the Eagles were preparing to bolt Philadelphia for Los Angeles or any other city that wanted an NFL team. "The Eagles aren't going anywhere," he declared. "They belong in Philadelphia and they are staying in Philadelphia."

As the owner and the man upstairs, it's unlikely that Lurie will ever get much credit from the ticket-buying public. His money and status just make it too hard for him to fit in. But even the most hard-nosed fans recognize that he has been a talented leader—especially compared to men like Tose, Braman, and Jerry Wolman.

Still, the fans' reaction to Lurie bothers Banner, who also would not rank among the region's most popular people even though he has helped produce a consistent winner. "I have to tell you, that's personally frustrating to me in a public-relations sense," Banner told *The Philadelphia Inquirer*. "I know this is controversial, but I don't think there's another owner who would have kept this team in Philadelphia for the economic deal we got on our stadium. I'm not trying to belittle the public contribution, but as it relates to what other cities did and other offers we had from other cities, I can't imagine many owners that would have come from someplace else and had the kind of loyalty that he demonstrated to these football fans and this city and the history of the franchise. I don't think anybody recognizes that. I don't think anybody thinks of that."

The Eagles didn't leave the Vet for the Linc until the 2003 season, but their on-field performance took a major step up in 1999 when they hired Green Bay offensive coordinator Andy Reid as head coach. While Reid had been instrumental in the development of Brett Favre and the mighty Packers offense, many of the pundits still wanted a more experienced coach to take over the talented but inconsistent Eagles. Lurie, however, was impressed with Reid's know-how, confidence, and organization.

"We needed somebody who had confidence and could take an organization that had been on a downhill slide and not only reverse that, but have a real focused plan on how to succeed in a big way," Lurie explained. "Not just talk, but a detailed, detailed plan."

When the team got off to a slow start under Reid, pressure grew as the fans and media began to feel that Lurie and Banner were little more than rich kids with a toy—a toy that they were about to break. But Lurie was convinced that Reid was the right man for the job, and he was not going to let any early difficulty dissuade him. He even went so far as to publicly reassert his position in an interview with *ESPN* magazine, promising that Reid had the ability to lead and would be a consistent winner.

Well into his second decade of owning the team, Lurie now knows that the franchise is on the right track. "I feel very good about this team and what we've been able to accomplish, but obviously we have more things to accomplish," Lurie said. "Our focus is to try to win Super Bowls."

The Eagles have played in the postseason eight times in 14 years during the Lurie-Banner era, posting a 9–8 record. Only the Indianapolis Colts have made more playoff appearances (11) than the Eagles in that span, and only the New England Patriots (17) and the Pittsburgh Steelers (12) have more playoff wins.

Lurie, Banner, and Reid have come to understand and truly believe in each other—even when the doubters have roared. During the 2006 season the Eagles lost five of six games during the middle of the season after an injury to McNabb, and tensions were high. But Reid told both men he had a handle on the situation and could fix the problem. He had their complete support, and that was all that was needed.

The Eagles turned things around to win the NFC East with a 10–6 record. During the postseason they edged the Giants 23–20 before suffering a heartbreaking 27–24 loss to the Saints before a roaring Superdome crowd.

The 2006 season may have ended there, but other NFC teams now know that if they are going to establish themselves as legitimate contenders for a chance at the Super Bowl, they are first going to have to get past a very formidable Eagles franchise.

FEAR AND LOATHING IN THE POINT SPREAD WARS

The wailing could be heard throughout the city after the Eagles' painful loss in Super Bowl XXXIX to the Patriots. This was the closest the team had come to an NFL Championship since winning the title in 1960.

But not everybody was crying. A late touchdown by Donovan McNabb had trimmed the deficit from 10 points to three, meaning that the Eagles had covered the point spread. The seven-point spread seemed simply too big, so even though most gamblers thought New England would win, the majority of the bettors both in Philadelphia and throughout the nation had the Eagles to cover. Huge amounts of money changed hands, and many gambling Eagles fans came up big winners.

Despite losing to the Patriots in Super Bowl XXXIX, McNabb and the Eagles at least made some members of the gambling community happy by covering the point spread with a late-game touchdown.

That Super Bowl cover marked the end of a brilliant postseason performance against the spread by the Eagles. They had been favored by seven and a half points in the divisional playoff against the Vikings and five and a half points against the Falcons in the NFC Championship game. They beat the Vikings 27–14 and then followed through with a 27–10 win over the Falcons. Three straight postseason covers paid for many a fine spring-break vacation for gamblers—or at least helped cover the tab from previous losses.

The Eagles did an outstanding job of rewarding their betting backers in a key late-season Monday night game in 2006. Needing wins in their final two games to secure a playoff spot, the Eagles went to Dallas to take on former Eagles wide receiver Terrell Owens, beleaguered coach Bill Parcells, and hot new quarterback Tony Romo. The Eagles were six and a half point underdogs at Texas Stadium, but they went into Dallas like they owned the place. Quarterback Jeff Garcia, playing for the injured Donovan McNabb, completed 15 of 23 passes for 238 yards, and Brian Westbrook ran for 122 yards as the Eagles rolled to an easy 23–7 win. They were ahead the entire game; Eagles supporters never even broke a sweat.

The 2003 season was memorable for a number of reasons, not all of them happy. The Eagles lost their third consecutive NFC Championship game, dropping an uninspired 14–3 contest as three and a half point favorites to the Panthers. However, during the regular season, the Eagles were point spread juggernauts. They won and covered nine straight games between week seven and week 15. Included in that streak were Monday night road wins over the Packers and the Dolphins as underdogs.

Of course it hasn't been all gravy for those who choose to bet on the Eagles. There have been many memorable spread defeats that have caused more than one supporter to wonder where the next rent payment will come from and how the gambling gods could be so cruel.

Going back to week six of the 2003 season is a painful memory for quite a few Eagles bettors. The Birds were favored by one and a half points as they traveled to Dallas. They had won two games in a row after a 0–2 start and appeared to be hitting their stride. It looked like the Eagles would get an easy win—and that they wouldn't even need the points.

But the Cowboys showed some life right from the opening kickoff. Philly coach Andy Reid tried to catch the Cowboys napping by attempting an onside kick to start the game. Not only did the Cowboys recover, but Randal Williams picked it up, easily escaped the grasp of the Eagles defenders, and then sprinted 37 yards to the end zone. The fans at Texas Stadium were delirious and sensed this was going to be their day.

The Eagles regained their balance and eventually took a 21–20 lead when Correll Buckhalter scored on a 20-yard run with 4:14 left. But the dejected Cowboys did not quit. They drove down the field, where the always-nervous Billy Cundiff delivered a game-winning 28-yard field goal with 1:11 left to secure a 23–21 win. Those one and a half points simply were not enough. The Eagles failed to cover by half a point.

Ray Rhodes presided over the Eagles for four years from 1995 through 1999. The era began auspiciously with a 10–6 season that saw the Eagles overpower Detroit 58–37 in a record-setting wild-card playoff game, but things soon went downhill. They made the playoffs again the following year but were blanked 14–0 in the wild-card game by the Niners. In 1997 they had a disappointing 6–9–1 record, and the Rhodes era ended after the 1998 season, when the Eagles finished in the NFC East cellar with a 3–13 record. But for betting fans, the most painful defeat of the Rhodes era actually came in a game the Eagles won. They defeated the Bengals 44–42 in week 14 as six-point favorites, leaving Philadelphia supporters wondering how their team could score 44 points and still not cover the spread.

One of the all-time most painful Eagles defeats came in week four of the 1985 season. The Giants came to the Vet as four and a half point favorites. New York had an excellent team that year that would go on to win the NFC East title before they were eliminated in the playoffs by the mighty Chicago Bears. While the Giants were not yet championship material—that would come the following year when they defeated the Broncos in Super Bowl XXI—they were vastly superior to Marion Campbell's Eagles. But on this day the Eagles played their hearts out and had a late lead before the Giants tied the game 10–10 to send it into overtime. The Eagles were four and a half point underdogs; it looked like they would still cover the spread, since the Giants would gladly go for a field goal if they got the ball into Eagles territory. But unfortunately for Eagles backers, the Giants never had to play a down on offense. Giants cornerback Elvis "Toast" Patterson picked off a Ron Jaworski pass and returned it for a game-winning touchdown—and stole a cover away from pained Eagles backers.

That's adding insult to injury.

THE AGONY OF DEFEAT

CRASH LANDING IN THE BIG EASY

It was the Eagles' year in 1980, and everyone in Philadelphia believed. After all, not only had they dominated the Cowboys 20–7 in the NFC Championship game, but during the regular season they had also beaten their Super Bowl opponents, the Raiders, 10–7.

This edition of the Raiders was not one of the NFL's all-time great teams. But somehow, even though *Sports Illustrated* had predicted that they would finish dead last in the AFC West, they made it into the postseason as a wild-card team. No wild-card team had ever made it to the Super Bowl before, let alone won it.

The Eagles believed they had a significant physical edge on the Raiders. They had sacked Raiders quarterback Jim Plunkett eight times in the two teams' first meeting, and there appeared to be little Raiders coach Tom Flores and his team could do to overcome them.

But the Raiders were not the least bit afraid of facing the Eagles in the Superdome. Flores figured all the pressure was on Dick Vermeil and his players. Nobody expected a wild-card team to win the Super Bowl. While Plunkett had enjoyed a renaissance season, the Eagles still didn't feel much fear about facing him—he wasn't exactly Johnny Unitas in his prime. Plunkett was a reclamation project.

The city of Philadelphia was on quite a roll at the time when it came to sports. The Phillies, who had won exactly zero World Series titles during their first 90 years in existence, had just beaten the Kansas City Royals in a six-game fall classic. The Flyers had gone to the 1980 Stanley Cup Finals against the New York Islanders, where they pushed the eventual four-time champions to six games. The Sixers went to the NBA Finals, where they lost to the Los Angeles Lakers in six games.

The Eagles, meanwhile, had hit their stride. They had improved in each of their first four seasons under Vermeil. After going 11–5 in 1979, qualifying for the playoffs, and beating the Chicago Bears in the wild-card game, 1980 saw them earn a 12–4 record and win the NFC East title. They dispatched the Vikings in the first round of the playoffs and got over an emotional hurdle to beat the Cowboys in the NFC Championship. But Vermeil made it clear that his team had significant business to take care of in New Orleans against the Raiders.

The Eagles did not seem comfortable in their role as favorites. While the Raiders were loose and seemingly worry free, the Eagles seemed to become more tense as the week of meetings with the media progressed. Vermeil's intensity, which had gotten so much out of the team all season, now seemed to drain them during Super Bowl week.

While the Eagles spent the majority of their time on the practice field, the Raiders were yukking it up on Bourbon Street. Flores fined his players more than $15,000 during Super Bowl week, a figure All-Pro guard Gene Upshaw thought was conservative. "We're not a bunch of choirboys and Boy Scouts," Upshaw told *Sports Illustrated*. "They say we're the halfway house of the NFL. Well, we live up to that image—every chance we get."

Instead of letting the Eagles take it to them the way they had during the regular season, the Raiders came out on an emotional high and took care of business. Eagles quarterback Ron Jaworski threw an interception to Raiders linebacker Rod Martin during the first series of the game, and Martin returned it to the Eagles' 30. That set up a two-yard Plunkett touchdown pass to wideout Cliff Branch before the game was even five minutes old.

Jaworski knew the Eagles had to respond—the quicker the

better—and he thought his team could tie the game two series later. The Eagles moved the ball steadily downfield and reached the Raiders 40. Speedy Rodney Parker got a step on the defense and Jaworski hit him with a bomb for an apparent touchdown. But wide receiver Harold Carmichael was called for motion on the other side of the field, and the play was called back. If the Eagles had lacked some emotion coming into the game, that play drained whatever they had left.

It was apparent that the Eagles had no gas left in the tank on the next series as Plunkett scrambled forward in the pocket and floated a pass to Kenny King in the left flat after he had gotten past the linebackers. King caught it in stride and held the ball like a loaf of bread in his left hand as he sprinted down the sideline for an 80-yard touchdown.

The play completely took the air out of the Eagles. The Raiders had a 14–0 lead, they had confidence, and they were able to dictate the pace for the rest of the game. The Eagles were dazed, confused, and emotionally drained.

The key to the Raiders' surprising turnaround from their previous game against Philadelphia was the Eagles' inability to stop the Oakland running game or get to Plunkett. During the two teams' regular-season meeting, Claude Humphrey had three and a half sacks against the Oakland quarterback, and as a team, the Eagles collected eight altogether on that day. But the only sack they recorded in the Super Bowl came when Plunkett scrambled out of trouble and dove for the line of scrimmage. He came up a yard short, so it was technically recorded as a sack.

The media had reminded the Oakland offensive line of their previous performance against the Eagles, and it only served to get them angry. "The first thing I heard when I was interviewed was about the eight sacks," said Raiders center Dave Dalby. "I got damn tired of hearing about it. We were not going to listen to that kind of talk after the Super Bowl."

The Eagles got on the board when Tony Franklin connected on a 30-yard field goal in the second quarter, but the Raiders were clearly in control as the game went to halftime. If the Eagles were going to mount a comeback, they would have to establish control at the start of the third quarter.

But it simply was not meant to be. The Raiders came out all business and went on a five-play, 76-yard drive that culminated with Plunkett's third touchdown pass of the game. This time he hit a twisting Cliff Branch with a 29-yard pass. With the score at 21–3, the game was all but over.

Martin and his teammates were whooping it up on defense. They were playing it loose and having fun. Nobody had expected anything from them, and now they were taking it to the powerful NFC Champions. Playing on instinct, Martin continued to dog Jaworski. He picked up his second interception on the next series, and Chris Bahr added a field goal to give Oakland a 21-point lead.

Jaworski was able to connect with tight end Keith Krepfle on an eight-yard touchdown pass in the fourth quarter, but that just made the score a bit more respectable. Oakland even added another field goal before taking home their second Super Bowl title. Plunkett had gained vindication after being branded as a bust following a tough run in New England and a two-year disaster in San Francisco.

While there was joy in Oakland, misery reigned in Philadelphia. Twenty years after their last championship in 1960, the city had once again been denied another title to celebrate.

Silver and Black Nightmares

Raiders owner Al Davis was all smiles after the game, enjoying one of his proudest moments as a result of his team's stellar performance. He told his players that their win over the Eagles was "the team's finest hour." He also had the pleasure of accepting the Vince Lombardi Trophy from his archrival, Commissioner Pete Rozelle.

Davis had been a thorn in Rozelle's side since the merger of the AFL and the NFL. Davis had been the most aggressive of the AFL owners in the years during which the two leagues had battled, and he was quite sure that the AFL could have won the war if peace had not been negotiated.

Their uncomfortable relationship came to the forefront as soon as the Raiders earned their spot in the Super Bowl with a win

Eagles quarterback Ron Jaworski was confounded by a Raiders defense that intercepted three of his passes in Super Bowl XV.

at San Diego in the AFC Championship. Both men held the other in contempt, and Davis made no attempt to hide his feelings. Rozelle acted with dignity in public, but it was clear that he had no fondness for Davis.

As Rozelle prepared to hand the trophy to Davis and congratulate him for his team's performance, television cameras were poised to record a confrontation rather than a coronation. But there were no fireworks—Rozelle honored the Raiders with the presentation and Davis accepted the trophy without rancor. However, if one looked closely at the tape, there was a slight sneer on Davis's smiling mug.

Davis had been somewhat confident of his team's chances for

winning the game going in, but it was clear that he considered the Eagles and head coach Dick Vermeil to be worthy opponents. Davis liked everything about the way Vermeil had gone about his business and prepared his team—and showed more respect for the Eagles coach than nearly any other opponent. He did, however, manage to throw out one zinger to *Sports Illustrated*.

"The man is true to what he believes and that was good enough to get them there," Davis said. "They're a damn tough team, don't make any mistake about that. The only thing is...well, it's tough to have a paramilitary group within the confines of a culture that isn't paramilitary. You have to adjust. Obviously he feels he doesn't have to. But you must realize that this was his first Super Bowl game."

The Raiders were able to use their offense to separate themselves from the Eagles, but it was their defense that really drove them. The key to that performance was the unexpectedly spectacular play of Martin, who set a Super Bowl record with three interceptions. He caught more of Jaworski's passes on Super Bowl Sunday than any Eagles players on the field, excepting Carmichael and running back Wilbert Montgomery.

Martin was one of the few Raiders who had not worked overtime on Bourbon Street prior to the game. Instead, he stayed in his hotel room and looked at film of the Eagles offense. He noticed that on plays in which the Eagles used two tight ends and also sent Carmichael wide, Jaworski almost always threw to the tight end on Martin's side of the field. That realization paid significant dividends on the third play of the game as Carmichael ran down the left sideline and tight end John Spagnola ran a hook pattern on Martin's side of the field. The linebacker dropped back and picked off Jaworski's wobbling pass.

That play put a charge into the Raiders sideline and lifted Martin's spirits considerably. He had enjoyed an outstanding week of practice, but that play gave him a major boost. He intercepted his second pass on another toss to Spagnola. He recognized the pattern, beat the tight end to the ball at the Raider 30, and went two yards before stepping out of bounds. Had he scored on that drive, they would have brought the score to 21–10 and perhaps changed the outcome of the game.

Martin's final interception came in the game's last minute. He picked off a desperation pass and returned it 25 yards to the Eagles 38. His three picks in the game exceeded his four-year career total of two and made him a contender for Super Bowl MVP honors. That award ultimately went to Plunkett, but that doesn't lessen Martin's impact in the biggest game in which he ever played.

MORE PAIN COMES WITH ANOTHER SHOT AT GLORY: SUPER BOWL XXXIX

After a brilliant season and a memorable run through the NFC playoffs, the Eagles finally made it back to the big game 24 years after their Super Bowl XV loss to the Raiders. This time they were seven-point underdogs as they took on the defending Super Bowl champions, the Patriots, a team that was going for its third world championship in four seasons.

Owens Comes Through

Controversy has been just about the only consistent aspect of Terrell Owens's career. He is obnoxious, self-centered, courageous, ridiculous, naïve, thought-provoking, talented, inconsistent—and many of these characteristics come to the fore within minutes of each other.

But on one particular occasion, Owens was on top of his game when the spotlight was brightest. He dominated in the Eagles' 24–21 loss to the Patriots in Super Bowl XXXIX. The Eagles' All-Pro receiver caught nine passes for 122 yards after rejecting his doctor's advice to sit out the game less than seven weeks after ankle surgery. "A lot of people in the world didn't believe I could play, but my faith alone—the power of prayer and the power of faith—carried me all the way," Owens said.

Three days after Owens had been injured in December, Dr. Mark Myerson inserted two screws in Owens's right ankle and a plate on the outside of the ankle. Owens was told after the surgery that he had only an outside chance of returning for the Super Bowl. But he still rehabbed vigorously, hoping to help Philadelphia win its first NFL title since 1960.

Terrell Owens celebrates after a 30-yard reception against the New England Patriots during the first quarter of Super Bowl XXXIX.

There were some who suspected that Owens would dress for the game and take the field just to fill the role of decoy. But that was hardly the case. Owens was a very busy man that day. He caught a seven-yard pass on Philadelphia's second play, and that should have told the Patriots all they needed to know. T.O. was ready to go.

Owens had a 30-yard catch-and-run later in the first quarter, setting up a first down at the Patriots' 8, but the Eagles failed to turn it into points. After that catch, Owens flapped his arms in bird-like fashion along the sideline. He also had a 36-yard reception in the fourth quarter, although he did not have a touchdown catch.

His effort was respected by the opposition. "For him to come back and play the way he played, I've got a lot of respect for him,"

Patriots linebacker Mike Vrabel said after the game.

Owens had no trouble running his patterns, gaining several yards after his catches. He seemed out of breath early on when he went to the sideline but didn't have to sit out plays.

Owens didn't have any receptions in the second quarter, as McNabb spread the ball around and had better success moving the offense, but he did have two catches during Philadelphia's game-tying scoring drive in the third quarter, giving him a total of six in the second half. "It's remarkable how he was able to come back and played so well for us," McNabb said.

Two days after the Eagles beat the Falcons in the NFC Championship game, Dr. Myerson had said that he couldn't clear Owens to play against the Patriots. But Owens insisted that he would be in the lineup—not just standing on the sideline leading cheers as he did in the last two regular-season games and the NFC title game—when Philadelphia made its first appearance in the Super Bowl since 1981.

This was the stage Owens had always wanted. The self-described playmaker knew he had to come through in the big game, and he indeed proved himself worthy.

Owens came into the game with confidence, leading Philadelphia's statistics for the season with 77 catches for 1,200 yards and 14 touchdowns. He invigorated the Eagles with his attitude, enthusiasm, and exceptional play, adding swagger to a team that desperately needed a personality.

With Owens in the lineup, the offense was extremely potent, averaging 25.4 points in 14 games. After Owens's injury, the Eagles had lost their last two regular-season games and the offense slowed considerably. However, that drop in offensive production was not entirely due to the loss of Owens; most of the Eagles starters took time off after the team clinched their status as the number one seeded team in the playoffs

The Eagles scored 27 points in each of their two playoff victories without Owens. But they couldn't pull out a win against the Patriots even with Owens spectacular performance. "They're an elite team," Owens said. "We played sloppy, but they made us play sloppy at times."

With a productive first year and a thriller of a performance in the Super Bowl, it seemed as if the marriage between Owens and the Eagles was in great shape. But it soon unraveled, and Owens's association with the Eagles quickly wound up on the rocks.

McNabb's Effort Falls Short

In the biggest game of his life, Donovan McNabb did everything but win.

Playing himself into a nauseated state of exhaustion, he threw for 357 yards and three touchdowns. The numbers were great, but as the Eagles tried to mount a miraculous comeback in the game's final moments, McNabb was unable to run the two-minute offense to perfection because he was sick to his stomach. He also tossed three costly interceptions and was bloodied by a Patriots defense that pressured him throughout the second half.

It's hard to criticize McNabb's effort in Philadelphia's 24–21 loss to New England. He played well enough to give Philly a shot. But at the end of the game, his poor performance—a sad ending to his best season ever—brought up the same question that had dogged him throughout his career: is he accurate enough to win a championship?

The numbers show that McNabb completed 59 percent of his passes in the Super Bowl, very similar statistics to those that he has posted throughout his career. But it's a rate that's low for a 28-year-old who's played his entire career in a quarterback-friendly offense. McNabb was responsible for Super Bowl XXXIX's best offensive plays, but he also gave the game its worst.

Even though McNabb nearly led the Eagles to a win against the two-time champion Patriots, he was never really on his game. He fumbled on the game's third play (although the call was overturned by a smart replay challenge by Eagles coach Andy Reid). On Philadelphia's third possession, he sliced New England apart with a 30-yard pass to Owens that gave the Eagles a first-and-goal at the 8. But on first down, he was dropped by Mike Vrabel for a 16-yard loss. On second down he tossed an air ball into the end zone that Asante Samuel intercepted. Fortunately, McNabb was bailed out by an illegal-contact penalty on Pats linebacker Roman

Donovan McNabb, who was reportedly ill during the game, reacts late in the fourth quarter against the Patriots during Super Bowl XXXIX.

Phifer. Instead of taking advantage of that reprieve, McNabb threw another pick, and this time it was even worse. He saw Brian Westbrook breaking free, but the pass was off course and Patriots defensive back Rodney Harrison intercepted.

"I don't think he [McNabb] got frustrated," said Eagles tight end L.J. Smith. "It just took him a little while to get in rhythm."

But when he did, it was spectacular. In the second quarter he found Todd Pinkston over the middle for 17 yards. He then found Pinkston again, deeper over the middle this time, for 40 yards. Then, on third-and-goal from the 6, he looked for Owens outside, came back inside, saw Smith walling off the defender with his big body, and delivered a perfect pass. The touchdown put the Eagles up 7–0.

The Eagles were dominating at that point, having outgained the Patriots 149 yards to 27, and they should have been up by more. But they had two turnovers and their lead was anything but secure. "We could have been blowing them out at that point," McNabb lamented.

McNabb's second half started the same as the first, overthrowing Pinkston and taking sacks. He again settled into a short zone, throwing on eight of 10 plays; he connected on seven of those passes, including a 10-yarder to Westbrook to tie the game at 14.

Reid was emphasizing McNabb's passing game because he had no confidence that his team's running game could get anything done against New England. He went almost exclusively to the pass—and that's exactly the kind of box into which Bill Belichick wanted to force the Eagles. There was no longer any surprise in the Philadelphia attack, and the vice started to tighten around McNabb. His passes lacked authority, and the pressure on him was clearly having an impact.

Still, in the fourth quarter, trailing by 10, McNabb hit Owens with a perfect pass for 36 yards. On the next play he threw to a wide-open Westbrook running a crossing pattern in the middle of the field. But McNabb's throw was high and well behind Westbrook—a simply awful pass—flying right into the arms of disaster. Patriots linebacker Tedy Bruschi made a diving interception.

Bruschi has punctuated his career with big plays in key moments, and he was true to form in this game. But, although Bruschi does deserve credit for his play, another look at the tape shows that McNabb's throw was unacceptably bad for any competent West Coast quarterback under similar circumstances—especially when you consider how strong some of McNabb's throws have been under more difficult conditions. His inconsistency was mind-boggling to long-suffering Eagles fans. His only response? "I'm not going to make excuses," he said.

McNabb had another chance in the fourth quarter against the Patriots defense, much like St. Louis quarterback Kurt Warner and Carolina's Jake Delhomme had had against the Patriots in previous Super Bowls. But McNabb and the Eagles just couldn't do it. Needing two scores to send the game into overtime after Adam Vinatieri gave the Patriots a 10-point lead with a 22-yard field goal with 8:40 to go in the fourth period, the Eagles painfully drove downfield in an effort to get the first score. McNabb threw an interception on the next series, but the Eagles forced the Patriots to punt and got the ball back with 5:40 left.

Hurry-up offense? Not this time. The Eagles played at a much slower pace than was expected. They were making progress down the field, but too much time was coming off the clock. The Eagles were huddling up between plays, receivers were walking back to the line of scrimmage, and as minute after minute disappeared, no one wearing green seemed to grasp the gravity of the situation or the simple fact that producing 10 points against the two-time champs is not easy. Finally, with 1:48 left in the game, McNabb hit Greg Lewis with a perfect 30-yard touchdown pass to close the gap to 24–21.

Reid, who was calling the plays and wasn't exactly on the field screaming for his players to show more urgency, said later, "We were trying to hurry it up, but things didn't work out that way." Owens would later let slip that McNabb was getting nauseated on the field—which would explain the lack of urgency to the attack.

The Patriots recovered David Akers's poor attempt at an onside kick, but the Eagles were able to get the ball back because

MISTAKES MADE

Why did the Eagles lose Super Bowl XXXIX? Because they made big mistakes at key moments. They gave up four sacks. They lost a fumble and blew defensive assignments. They also had three interceptions. Those mistakes were the difference between winning and losing. The Eagles hung close with the defending Super Bowl champs, but it was not enough.

"You can't throw it to them [the Patriots]," said former Eagles offensive coordinator Brad Childress, who would later go on to become the head coach of the Vikings. "It's kind of a fundamental thing."

Ironically, the Eagles had been great on fundamentals during the regular season. They forced mistakes and they did not make them. That's how they won 13 games, earned the number one seed in the NFC, and made it through the playoffs. During the regular season, few teams took better care of the ball than the Eagles. For the season, they had only 22 giveaways—11 picks and 11 lost fumbles—finishing seventh in that category. And three of those turnovers came in a meaningless season finale against Cincinnati. McNabb threw only eight interceptions in 2004 and found his receivers in the end zone 31 times. In a league where a 2:1 touchdown-to-interception ratio is considered as difficult to achieve as finding the Holy Grail, McNabb nearly reached the 4:1 mark.

But in the Super Bowl it was almost as if a different bunch of players had donned Eagles uniforms. McNabb was sacked on the team's first possession and threw three picks—three interceptions in one game, after throwing only eight all season long.

The Eagles had an explanation. It even made sense. But it did nothing to take away the pain. "They're a good team that forces turnovers. That's what they do," wide receiver Freddie Mitchell told the media after the game. "We expect that, and we try to limit that. But tonight, we didn't do it."

The Patriots got the proper amount of respect from the Eagles before and after the game. But it was clear that the Eagles had simply failed to play at their best.

"We made mistakes," said tight end L.J. Smith. "They took advantage of those mistakes. That's what good teams do. They make you pay when you make a mistake."

The 2004 season was a great one for McNabb. He rolled through the regular season and was on his game in the divisional playoff against Minnesota and the NFC Championship game against Atlanta. He handled Super Bowl week with aplomb. He even played very well—at least for short bursts—in the game. But in the end he made mistakes that would haunt him.

"Three interceptions. I don't look at the touchdowns. I don't look at any of that," said McNabb, who threw for 357 yards and three touchdowns. "As the quarterback, you want to make sure you take care of the ball. Turnovers kill you, and they hurt us against the Pats."

The hurt will remain for McNabb, his teammates, his coaches, and Eagles fans until the day finally comes when they can claim the Vince Lombardi Trophy.

Coach Reid has saved his last two time outs. The Eagles took possession at their own 4-yard line with only 46 seconds to go.

Harrison recorded his second interception of the game with nine seconds left, but it was too little too late. Final score: New England 24, Philadelphia 21.

After three successive NFC Championship losses, McNabb had upgraded his level of play to get his team to the Super Bowl. But once he got there, although he had moments of greatness, he could not do the job consistently. He threw for more touchdowns and yardage than Tom Brady and did things to the New England defense that Peyton Manning wouldn't be able to do for another two years. But he needs another opportunity on the big stage to prove that he can do it from start to finish and put his name up there with the great quarterbacks of the game.

Reid knew that his quarterback had given his all and that the effort was there. "He battled his heart out on the field," Reid said. "He gave it everything he had." But Reid also knew that he needed more from his quarterback than he got on that day—it just wasn't enough to overcome the power of the Patriots dynasty. That's what Belichick's team became after registering this 24–21 win, its third title in four years.

It was a game that had everything, but one that ultimately left a very poor taste in McNabb's mouth.

STEPPED ON BY THE GIANTS

Bill Parcells has won two Super Bowls and is one of the most memorable coaches the game has ever known. He is familiar to most football fans as a demanding head coach with an acerbic tongue. When talking with the press during the season, it seems as if Parcells enjoys the give-and-take about as much as he would a root canal—but his answers show that he's the one with the drill in his hand.

Parcells won two Super Bowls as head coach of the Giants, went to another as the head coach of the Patriots, got to the AFC title game as boss of the Jets, and led the Cowboys to multiple playoff appearances. But if you ask him when he knew that he was going to make a name for himself in pro football, he'll tell you it came during the 1981 season against the Eagles.

At the time Parcells was not yet a head coach. He was the defensive coordinator and linebacker coach for the Giants, freshly hired by head coach Ray Perkins. The Giants were just about to emerge from 18 years without a playoff appearance, but they had a lot of work to do in order to improve their defense. They had ranked 27th (out of 28 teams) in defense in 1980, and had given up 425 points. Perkins charged Parcells with the responsibility of giving him both a linebacker crew he could depend on and a solid defense.

A case can be made that Parcells came in with a stacked hand, as the Giants used their number two overall pick in the draft to take Lawrence Taylor. As soon as he took the field, the highly touted linebacker from the University of North Carolina became "L.T."—a hurricane who destroyed everything in his path. L.T. had it all: talent, aggressiveness, speed, natural strength, and an unquestioned will to win, and he adjusted to the NFL in no time. In addition to Taylor, Parcells also had a crew of talented linebackers to work with in Harry Carson, Brad Van Pelt, and Brian Kelley. On offense he had a young but unproven quarterback named Phil Simms.

The Giants were able to show improvement right away. Taylor, of course, had an enormous impact immediately, with nine and a half sacks as a rookie along with 94 solo tackles and 39 assists. Taylor and Parcells built a special relationship, and as good as the linebacker already was, his coach brought more out of him.

Still, Parcells wasn't sure that he truly belonged in the NFL until the Giants beat the Eagles in a week 12 game at Veterans Stadium.Vermeil's team had been to the Super Bowl the year before and brought a 9–2 record into this late-season home game against the Giants. The Eagles had put away New York 24–10 in their week one meeting in the Meadowlands. The Giants now faced the crossroads of their season in a game that appeared to have blowout loss stamped all over it. They had shown some improvement in the first half of the year after beating teams like the Cardinals, Falcons, and Seahawks, but they were 5–6 when they bused into Philadelphia via the Jersey Turnpike and had lost three games in a row.

The Eagles had the potential to bury the Giants and ruin their chances for a memorable season. Perkins knew he had to make a change in his lineup, so he named Scott Brunner as his starting quarterback, sending Simms to the bench. The Giants came through with their best game of the season, finding a way to beat the Eagles 20–10.

For three quarters the Giants managed to trade punches with the Eagles; at the start of the fourth they were still standing, with the score tied 10–10. Place-kicker Joe Danelo gave the Giants the lead with a 30-yard field goal; Parcells's defense then put the game away when cornerback Terry Jackson picked off a Jaworski pass and returned it 32 yards for the clinching touchdown.

Not only did this turn out to be a pivotal game for New York—they would win three of their last four to make the playoffs—it also hurt the Eagles badly. After dominating the NFC for nearly two full seasons, the loss to the Giants gave the Eagles a feeling of insecurity. Instead of letting the loss roll off their backs and moving on, Philadelphia next lost three tough road games (to Miami, Washington, and Dallas) before rolling St. Louis 38–0 in their season finale. Meanwhile, the Giants' 13–10 overtime win over the Cowboys in their own season finale earned them a spot in the postseason. They would be matched once again with the

TOM BRADY'S LEGACY

Tom Brady may not have been selected in the first round of the NFL draft, but none of that seems to matter now when looking back over his historic career, which is still playing out in the biggest games in the NFL. He has used his skill, intelligence, and confidence to overcome his lack of physical gifts, becoming one of the most dominating quarterbacks in NFL history.

Brady was not the MVP in the Patriots Super Bowl win over the Eagles (wide receiver Deion Branch earned that award), but he was the difference-maker when the game was on the line. He led the Patriots on touchdown drives at the end of the first half and the start of the second that gave them control against the Philadelphia Eagles in a 24–21 victory.

"I felt I was very prepared tonight, more so than ever before," Brady said. "I wish we had gotten things going a little quicker, but I knew I was looking in the right places."

If there was a moment that defined the magic of Brady that day, it came late in the first half on a play that easily could have put the Patriots in a 14–0 hole at intermission. On second-and-goal from the 4, Brady dropped back and looked to his right and then back over the middle. With the Eagles' pass rush closing in, he saw David Givens standing on the far right side of the end zone. Cornerback Lito Sheppard relaxed slightly because he didn't think Brady could get the ball to Givens. Brady threw a sidearm laser about 20 yards across the field that arrived just before Sheppard did.

"Tom threw it right where he had to throw it," Givens said. "I looked up and it hit me exactly where I wanted it. Tom placed the ball right on the money." There was no other choice. Anything less, and Sheppard would have had an easy pick—and a sure touchdown unless Givens could have caught him from behind.

"The touchdown to Givens, that was about his third read on the play down there," Belichick said. "That was an outstanding play, because he just read his progression all the way out and made a great read and a throw to Givens."

On their next drive the Patriots set the tone for the second half. They found their rhythm with a nine-play, 69-yard drive that began with a safe, simple route to Branch for eight yards. Branch caught three more passes, one of them on third-and-10. The drive ended with a great read and another great throw, this time to linebacker Mike Vrabel, who had lined up as a tight end and fought through a hold by defensive end Jevon Kearse to make a juggling catch.

Brady made one big mistake that could have turned out huge. With the Patriots trailing 7–0, he drove them 82 yards in seven plays to the 54. But on a play-action fake to Kevin Faulk, Brady got too close to his running back and bumped into him. The ball fell to the ground and the Eagles recovered.

But Brady made no mistakes when the game was on the line. When the Eagles started to blitz, he used a screen pass to Dillon. Brady finished with 23 completions on 33 attempts for 236 yards and two touchdowns, with no interceptions.

He also got to walk off the field in Jacksonville and into history. His name stands with those of Terry Bradshaw, Joe Montana, and Troy Aikman as the only quarterbacks in NFL history to win three or more Super Bowl titles.

Eagles—a meeting that inspired both pride and fear in Parcells.

The Giants used a quick start to take a 20–0 first quarter lead and then went on to beat the Eagles 27–21. "That was the best part of the season for us, because we beat the Eagles in the playoffs," Parcells later recalled in his autobiography, aptly entitled *Parcells: A Biography*. "As a coach, you have to set goals, whether you vocalize them or not. And I was obsessed with beating the Eagles. All of the rivalries in the NFC East were big ones, but the most important one to me was with the Eagles. They had been to the Super Bowl the year before and they were our measuring stick."

Parcells had great respect for Jaworski and Carmichael, but it was Montgomery who was his primary focus. From Parcells's perspective, Montgomery was a talented back with speed, quickness, and agility, but it was his toughness that was his best characteristic. "He was as tough a running back as there was in the league at that time," Parcells said. "Our guys called him Timex, because he could take a licking and keep on ticking."

Beating the Eagles twice in Philadelphia in the same season proved to Parcells that his team was coming into their own and that he was a worthy NFL coach. His big break came a year later when Perkins resigned at the end of the 1982 season to take over for Bear Bryant as the head coach at the University of Alabama.

New York general manager George Young hired Parcells as his new head coach—and a legend was born.

Parcells has clearly demonstrated that he has what it takes to be one of the game's greatest coaches. But like everyone else, he had to prove himself—and he wasn't even really sure that he belonged in the game until the Giants beat the Eagles late in the 1981 season.

THE BUCS TAKE IT UP A NOTCH

The Eagles thought they were about to take an inevitable step forward as they entered the 2002 playoffs. After losing the 2001 NFC Championship game on the road to a very powerful St. Louis Rams team, the Eagles had the home-field advantage they wanted.

Philadelphia, Tampa Bay, and Green Bay had all finished with 12–4 records in 2002, but the Eagles earned a bye and home-field advantage throughout the playoffs based on an 11–1 record against conference foes. They won their divisional playoff game against Atlanta without much of a struggle; the Eagles defense shut down speedy quarterback Michael Vick with a systematic 20–6 victory and then moved on to the NFC Championship game.

As they prepared for the Bucs, Eagles supporters were almost deliriously optimistic. Not only had the warm-weather Bucs won only one game in their history when the temperature was below 40 degrees (against the Bears in their regular-season finale less than a month earlier), but they were also venturing into Philadelphia for the last game ever to be played at the Vet. Fans who had long before earned a reputation for being among the least congenial spectators in all of sports were not about to start using Emily Post manners for this Veterans Stadium swan song.

The Bucs had a great defense, with players like Derrick Brooks, Simeon Rice, Warren Sapp, John Lynch, and Ronde Barber, but the offense was pedestrian. The Eagles had supposedly paid their dues, gaining the necessary experience to advance to the Super Bowl by playing in the NFC Championship game the year before. The Bucs were expected to get their experience at the Vet and then have a better chance of advancing the following year.

Donovan McNabb was harassed by the defense of Tampa Bay Buccaneers, including Simeon Rice, right, and Greg Spires (94), all day during the NFC Championship game at Veterans Stadium in January 2003.

That's how the theory went, anyway. But it seems nobody told Bucs coach Jon Gruden or his players.

The game got off to a brilliant start when Eagles return specialist Brian Mitchell ran the opening kickoff back for 71 yards to the Tampa Bay 26. When Duce Staley then pounded the ball in from the 20, the Eagles were in the end zone less than a minute into the game.

Eagles fans were thinking rout. But Gruden remained extremely confident. He had sensed his team was ready to play a huge game, and the early touchdown against them did not diminish the confidence on the sideline. "You worry about that because a big play early is definitely a problem," Gruden recalled. "But there was no thought that this was not going to be our day. Just a little bump in the road." The Buc defense gave up little else that day.

The Eagles led 7–3 after allowing a 48-yard field goal by Martin Gramatica. Eagles right cornerback Bobby Taylor then intercepted a Brad Johnson pass to put Philadelphia in position to stretch their lead, but they were unable to move the ball and punter Lee Johnson pinned the Bucs in at the 5-yard line.

The Eagles defense may have smelled more blood, but the Bucs would have none of it. The offensive line started to assert itself, giving Brad Johnson some time in the pocket. He found Joe Jurevicius on a crossing pattern, and the lanky receiver took the ball 71 yards. Mike Alstott would score two plays later, giving the Bucs a 10–7 lead and the confidence to finish the game with a full head of steam.

As the game went on, Brad Johnson lost his fear of playing in the Vet against a ferocious defense. The Bucs were controlling Jim Johnson's pressure defense, allowing their veteran quarterback to complete 20 of 33 passes for 259 yards. The Bucs went with a no-huddle offense and often used a quick count, leaving the Eagles defense off balance.

The Bucs took the lead for good in the second quarter. After the Eagles tied it 10–10 on a David Akers 30-yard field goal, Brad Johnson found Keyshawn Johnson with a nine-yard touchdown pass. The Eagles tried to respond before halftime when they drove onto the Bucs' side of the field, but Tampa Bay defensive end Simeon Rice sacked his hometown buddy McNabb, forcing a fumble, and Rice recovered. Rice and McNabb had played together at Mt. Carmel High School in Chicago just a few years earlier. The Eagles found themselves trailing at halftime; this was especially troubling because they had had solid field position throughout the first half. Tampa Bay seized the momentum in the third quarter when they stretched their lead to 20–10 on another Gramatica field goal. The game was over when Barber intercepted a pass intended for Antonio "Buttons" Freeman and returned it 92 yards for a score.

McNabb was harassed throughout the game. He completed only 26 of 49 passes for 243 yards; he also fumbled twice. Although he blamed himself, it was not entirely McNabb's fault. The Bucs simply whipped the Eagles in almost every facet of the game.

The depression was palpable in the Eagles locker room; they had truly wanted to close the Vet in style by earning a spot in Super Bowl XXXVII. Instead, the Bucs had their tickets punched; they knew they had gotten over the hump.

"You wait for a chance to play in the Super Bowl all your life," said Alstott. "The circumstances were tough because Philadelphia had a great team and they were playing at home. But we were not about to give ourselves any excuse. Now we get to play in the Super Bowl. Nobody will like us in that game either, but we will show up."

The Bucs had some serious advantages over the Raiders when they met in the Super Bowl, the most notable of which was their young, strong, swift defense. It also didn't hurt that Gruden was one year removed from coaching the Raiders and was therefore familiar with all of their habits and weaknesses. The Bucs punished the Raiders 48–21 at Qualcomm Stadium in San Diego, and they were laughing and joking at press conferences after the game.

"Truthfully speaking, we all felt that once we got past Philly, we weren't about to lose this game," said Sapp. "That was a much bigger test for us—going to the Vet, in front of those fans, against that team. We knew if we could win that one, we were not about to let it slip through our fingers here."

The Eagles could take some comfort from the defeat, since at least some of the Bucs thought that Philly was better than the vanquished Raiders. But it was cold comfort for a very disappointed team that would not find relief until the end of the 2004 season, when they finally made it to the Super Bowl.

SOMEBODY'S WATCHING YOU

FAMOUS EAGLES FANS

One way of judging a team's popularity is by noting its celebrity fans. The Eagles are truly a blue-collar team that attracts hard-nosed, tough-minded fans who can break off one-liners as quickly as David Letterman (a Colts fan, by the way). However, several big-time performers and one notable author carry Eagles affiliations—and so did a princess who once lit up the world's stage.

Will Smith

The one-time Fresh Prince of Bel-Air is true to the lyrics of his show's opening theme song: born and raised in Philadelphia, he is a big-time fan of all of Philly's sports teams. The Eagles and the Sixers have always been his favorites, and none of that has changed since he reached megastar status. Smith has a collection of vintage sports jerseys, but the ones he likes best are his Eagles jerseys. Smith and his wife, Jada Pinkett-Smith, may not be in the end zone seats at the Linc, but his heart is with the team, and when the Eagles are winning, he is a much happier guy than when they are losing.

Seth Green

This talented young actor, best known for his role as Dr. Evil's son in Mike Myers's *Austin Powers* movies, has a strong taste for Eagles green and has been a lifelong fan. Green, who has a long and impressive film resume, has never been shy about his appreciation of and love for the team.

Holly Robinson Peete

Perhaps the most die-hard Eagles fan among celebrities, Robinson Peete took her love of the team to the extreme when she married one-time Eagles quarterback Rodney Peete. The two have been married since 1995 and have four children. Robinson Peete was born in Philadelphia and lived there until the age of 10 before moving with her family to Los Angeles. The one-time star of *21 Jump Street* has no use for the Cowboys, Giants, or Redskins, and takes as much joy from their defeats as she does from Eagles victories.

James Michener

This prolific author from Bucks County, Pennsylvania, won the Pulitzer Prize for *Tales of the South Pacific* in 1948 and is well known for penning lengthy sagas describing generations of families in far-off locations. Most of his work was fiction, but in 1976 he also wrote the well-received *Sports in America*, a comprehensive examination of sports in American life. Michener was a huge sports fan and his team of choice was—surprise!—the University of Texas women's basketball team. But he was also proud of his Pennsylvania roots and never lost his appreciation for the Eagles. Michener died in 1997.

Tommy Lasorda

This former manager of baseball's Dodgers franchise is one of the loudest and most cocky individuals in all of sports, and he's more than happy to take on the cause of anyone who's willing to pay him—remember how he used to hawk Slim Fast products? Lasorda has been a name-dropper supreme, telling all who will listen about how stars like Frank Sinatra and Don Rickles were his pals. But he is true to his Norristown, Pennsylvania, roots and loves Philadelphia teams. While he was particularly close to former Villanova basketball coach Rollie Massimino, he also loves football and the Eagles.

Kobe Bryant

This Lakers star is, of course, a Philadelphia native. While he spent many of his formative years outside of the country while his father, Joe "Jellybean" Bryant, pursued his basketball career in Europe, Kobe came back to Philadelphia during his teenage years and honed his basketball skills at Lower Merion High School in Ardmore, Pennsylvania (a suburb of Philadelphia). While he has been booed in some of his trips back to Philly to play the Sixers, he still loves Philadelphia fans. "They know what it's all about and they are so passionate," Bryant said. "Whether it's the Sixers, Flyers, Eagles, or Phillies, they are into it. I absolutely love Philadelphia and love those fans."

Bob Saget

Many know him as the genial Danny Tanner from the 1980s sitcom *Full House,* and many more would recognize him as the host of *America's Funniest Home Videos.* But while Saget may appear wholesome and warm in his role as a television personality, he is downright raunchy as a stand-up comedian and makes no apologies for his use of blue humor. In the film *The Aristocrats*, Saget's telling of the classic dirty joke by the same name is probably the raunchiest of the dozens of versions performed by the many comedians who appear in the film.

Saget was born in Philadelphia in 1956 and went to Temple University. He has been an Eagles fan through the best and the worst of times.

Bill Cosby

This American institution wears his hometown on his sleeve, literally and figuratively. Cosby grew up in Philadelphia and played both high school and college football in the city. He was a running back at Temple University and loved football, but realized his future was on the comedy circuit rather than in the NFL. He left Temple after his sophomore year. His parents may not have approved, but it seems apparent now that he made the right choice. Cosby has maintained strong ties with Temple and has been particularly close to former Owls basketball coach John Chaney. Cosby loves sports and football in particular. The Eagles have been his team since childhood, and they remain a key part of his life as a sports fan.

Danny Bonaduce

Former child star Danny Bonaduce has battled off-screen problems since his early days as the star of the hit TV series *The Partridge Family*, but it is hard to find an entertainer with more resiliency. Bonaduce has been a talk-radio host in multiple cities and starred in reality television. He has also developed a niche for himself as a boxing wannabe, taking on other former child stars like Donny Osmond and Barry Williams (*The Brady Bunch*) and winning each time. Bonaduce is consumed with himself and his own issues and only has a slight affiliation with the Eagles.

Toni Basil

This Philadelphia native and singer of the one-hit wonder song "Mickey" was once a cheerleader, and she said the energy she used while cheering gave her an edge when she became a singer. Sadly, her career never produced any other hit songs. But she remains a big fan of the Eagles in particular and of all Philadelphia teams.

Kevin Bacon

Known nearly as well for the movie trivia game "Six Degrees of Kevin Bacon" as he is for his prolific film career, Bacon is a man of varied interests. In addition to an acting career that has seen him star in *Footloose*, *Stir of Echoes*, *JFK*, *Wild Things*, *The River Wild*, *Sleepers*, *My Dog Skip*, and *Apollo 13*, the Philadelphia native has a second career as a musician alongside his brother, Michael. Their group, The Bacon Brothers, has been touring since 2001. Despite his hectic work schedule—not to mention raising a family with his wife, actress Kyra Sedgwick—Bacon still continues to love the Eagles and roots for them with passion and emotion.

Adam Sandler

Despite growing up in Manchester, New Hampshire, Sandler proudly touts his New York allegiance. When it comes

SECTION 700—THE NEST OF DEATH

In the upper deck of what used to be Veterans Stadium, there was once a section of fans that made "The Dawg Pound" in Cleveland look like a playpen for cuddly puppies. This was Section 700, the so-called "Nest of Death," where loyalty to the Eagles was the only qualification. This is where decency and civility went to die. But it was also a group that put everything it had in its collective soul on display for all to see and hear.

When the Eagles left the Vet at the end of the 2002 season, many writers around the NFL took the opportunity to look back at the havoc that had been caused by the fans of Section 700. But strangely, there seemed to be nearly as much veneration of the Section 700 fans as there was disgust. Thom Loverro of *The Washington Times* wrote a scathing column upon the Redskins' last visit to the Vet detailing many of the incidents that had taken place there over the years, including the booing of Santa Claus (which actually occurred at Franklin Field) and Irvin's painful exit. But when he wrote about the Redskins' experiences at the Vet, the piece turned nostalgic. He pointed out that Redskins fans gave as good as they got at the Vet and that Washington fans had even won the grudging respect of the Eagles fans who inhabited the Nest.

to football, he is a die-hard Jets fan, which means he also despises the New England Patriots. When the Pats met the Eagles in Super Bowl XXXIX in Jacksonville, Sandler was unable to stomach the idea of rooting for the Pats. "I'm adopting the Eagles," Sandler said. "I may not be an Eagles fan, but on Super Bowl Sunday, I'm with them. I just can't go with the Pats under any circumstances."

Sylvester Stallone

Stallone has long been an Eagles supporter. How could Rocky root for anyone else? Stallone and his famous character have been associated with Philadelphia for more than 30 years, and when the movie *Rocky Balboa* came out in 2006, he promoted the film by making his first publicity appearance for it during the middle of a *Monday Night Football* game between the Eagles and the Panthers. He was greeted by raucous cheers from the Philadelphia faithful.

Tara Reid

This former Hollywood sex kitten may be on the downside of a brief career, but she's a huge Eagles fan. While she has made the gossip sheets for her dating habits—Patriots quarterback Tom Brady, Ravens quarterback Kyle Boller, and Giants tight end Jeremy Shockey are among the notches on her belt—she also loves football and has been rooting for the Eagles since childhood. Reid grew up in Wyckoff, New Jersey, just a short distance from Philadelphia, and has been known to sport her Eagles jersey in public on many occasions.

Diana, Princess of Wales

No, we're not joking. Before her tragic death in 1997, Diana developed a fondness for the Eagles when they played a preseason game in London against the Cleveland Browns in 1989. She was given an Eagles jersey before the game, a 17–13 Philadelphia victory, and she actually wore it on occasion afterward. It was said that she developed a bit of a crush on Eagles quarterback Randall Cunningham.

ROWDY EAGLES FANS

Fan: Short for *fanatic*, as in losing all control and decorum in support of a sports team.

In the pantheon of North American sports, there are many great examples of passionate fandom. But there can be no doubt that professional football holds the highest spot on the totem poll. Passion is the watchword throughout the league, and more than a dozen cities can make a case for having the best fans in the sport. But when the qualities in question are passion, intelligence, and creativity, Philadelphia holds the edge over Chicago, New York, Washington, and Dallas.

The infamous story of Eagles fans booing Santa Claus in a

1968 game against the Vikings at Franklin Field has been used to peg the group as insufferable. But let's look at the facts. The Eagles had hired an actor to dress up as Santa Claus and parade around Franklin Field's running track exterior, waving to fans and wishing them a Merry Christmas. But Santa didn't show, and the Eagles went looking for an alternative. Frank Olivo was sitting in the stands rooting for the Eagles—while wearing a Santa suit. Eagles officials explained their plight and asked Olivo to step in.

Olivo was a great sport and decided to do it. But he had no acting skills and did not sport the rotund form that everyone expects in a Claus. Instead of rallying around Santa, fans saw what the Eagles organization was offering up and started booing and raining down snowballs. Luckily Olivo escaped the barrage without injury.

Fans are vociferous and physical in Philadelphia, and snowballs have not been the only projectiles. Fans have been known to throw batteries, rocks, and crushed beer cans. The worst example of the fans taking it too far may have been in a 1989 game against Dallas when Eagles fans started launching snowballs loaded with debris at Cowboys coach Jimmy Johnson. While the well-coiffed one did not get hit, back judge Al Jury was knocked down by a blow to the head. Owner Norman Braman was disgusted and embarrassed by the showing and immediately banned beer sales. But that measure was not enough, and incidents continued.

The worst of those occurred during a 1998 *Monday Night Football* game when an estimated 60 fights broke out in the stands. The Vet had become a war zone, and owner Jeffrey Lurie, who had bought the team from Braman, wanted to tone down the dysfunctional atmosphere. Lurie met with city officials to craft an agreement to create a courtroom in the basement of Veterans Stadium with hard-nosed judge Seamus McCaffery running the show. McCaffery administered justice on an immediate basis and was not afraid to impose stiff fines or force fans to give up their season tickets when necessary. "Eagle Court" was a definite success. Incidents of violence and fan misbehavior went down considerably, allowing the Vet to become a much more decent place to attend games.

A bare-chested Eagles fan cheers his team on against the Dallas Cowboys during a December 1995 game in Philadelphia. Temperatures were frigid as the Eagles defeated the Cowboys 20–17.

FIELD OF DOOM

Players like playing on grass and they hate playing on artificial turf. This has been the mantra of both football and baseball players since artificial turf was first introduced at Houston's Astrodome, built in 1965.

Over the years many advances have been made to this ersatz "grass," to the point where the FieldTurf product currently used in places like Seattle and New England is now widely accepted without issue. But it took a long time for artificial turf to progress to the point where it was no longer a legitimate point of controversy. And there was perhaps no field more dangerous than the artificial surface installed at the Vet.

It was bad for the Phillies when they played 81 home games there every season, but it was nearly unconscionable for the Eagles. The one thing that was unanimous in the NFL was that the turf in Philadelphia was the worst in the league.

Many injuries throughout the Eagles' 32 years at the Vet have been blamed on the turf, but the worst ever was the double kneecapping suffered by Wendell Davis of the Chicago Bears early in the 1993 season. Davis, the Bears' go-to receiver at the time, was going over the middle when he reversed and attempted to jump for a pass. He twisted to change direction, his shoes became locked to the turf, and he could barely get off the ground. He crumpled to the turf with the certain knowledge that something awful had happened—and he was right. He had ruptured the patellar tendons in both knees, and the results were catastrophic. His kneecaps, no longer secured in place by the tendons, were no longer in their proper place; they had moved up into his thighs.

Eagles owner Norman Braman was horrified, as were the Eagles players. Braman hired Kansas City's George Toma, the guru of groundskeepers, as a consultant in an attempt to address the problem. Toma didn't mince words after he and Braman inspected the Veterans Stadium field together for more than an hour. "There's a big problem there," Toma said. "And [Braman] was clearly concerned when we went over those problems. I give him a lot of credit."

Toma pointed out that the turf's major problems—ridges, gaps, and uneven surfaces—stemmed from the original installation in 1988. "I am not against artificial turf, but I'm sure as hell against poor artificial turf installations," Toma said. "That is a problem with some of these turfs. You can have problems from Day

One if the turf is not put in right. I'm probably the only man who has worked on every artificial turf, and I've seen fields that were so bad from Day One."

Toma pointed out that there was plenty of blame to go around. "There are a lot of bad groundskeepers," Toma said. "I get so mad at groundskeepers around the country who basically don't give a damn. Artificial turf has to be maintained as much as grass. If it isn't properly maintained, you can get some serious problems."

After Davis's gruesome injury, Eagles safety Rich Miano compared the Veterans Stadium experience to the hazards of working in an asbestos factory. Davis concurred. After his injury he was confined to a wheelchair for a month with both legs in casts. He also suffered psychological scars from the memory of looking down at his legs as he lay in pain on the Veterans Stadium turf. "My kneecaps were missing," Davis said. "You just don't get over that."

"I am very proud of what we were able to accomplish," McCaffery said. "Things were not safe for fans who paid to watch a football game. There's nothing wrong with fans who care about their team. But they have to know they can't take it over the line. People are responsible for their own behavior when they are out in society—whether they are at a football game, a movie theater, or a library. If they don't control their behavior, than society has to control them. That's what we were able to do."

While inappropriate incidents became far less frequent under McCaffery, they weren't wiped out completely. Dallas wide receiver Michael Irvin saw his NFL career come to an end when he took a hard hit and fell head first into the contentious turf at the Vet in December 1999. As he lay motionless and was then taken off the field by an ambulance, Eagles fans booed loudly. Irvin, who was voted into the Pro Football Hall of Fame in 2007, was one of the most flamboyant and aggravating receivers ever to set foot in the Vet, but the idea of booing him when it appeared that he had suffered a serious injury that could rob him of his ability to walk and use his extremities was simply atrocious. The incident left city officials, team management, players, and broadcasters with the unmistakable taste of embarrassment, anger, and humiliation in their mouths. Philadelphia Mayor Ed Rendell, an Eagles season ticket holder, called the fans "idiots" for booing a seriously injured player, and prominent Philadelphia columnists took the fans to task in print. Cowboys running back Emmitt Smith labeled the booing fans as "ignorant" and said he was disgusted by what he heard.

Irvin had suffered a herniated disc. His doctors also discovered that he had been born with a narrow spinal cord and was, therefore, more susceptible to serious spinal injuries. This discovery was the main reason behind his decision to retire, a move that ended one of the most successful and scandalous careers in Cowboys history.

That day may have been the nadir as far as Eagles fan behavior is concerned. When the team moved to Lincoln Financial Field, the atmosphere became far more tolerable—nothing resembling warm and fuzzy, but significantly better—and "Eagle Court" was discontinued. Some of the fans actions can be viewed as nothing short of hooliganism, but nobody can accuse Philadelphia fans of lacking passion for their teams. In an era of free agency and fast money for unproven players, particularly rookies, Philadelphia fans just want to make sure their players care about winning as much as they do. When players come to Philly who are more interested in individual achievements than in representing the team or the city well, they are often sent home.

Just ask Terrell Owens. While many called him a hero after his performance against the Patriots in Super Bowl XXXIX, in the end he turned out to be little more than a money-grubbing, me-first performer with delusions of grandeur. Coach Andy Reid wouldn't abide it, and neither would the Philadelphia fans, who have been waiting not-so-patiently for the team's first championship since 1960.

PAIN AND SUFFERING

THE UNTIMELY DEATH OF JEROME BROWN

The heart and soul of the Philadelphia defense was taken away in a cruel accident on June 25, 1992. Jerome Brown anchored the defensive line for Buddy Ryan's attacking defense, but he was so much more than a physical presence. He described himself as a "big old kid," but he was the leader of a locker room that had nothing but love and respect for him. He was known for his deftly fired digs, which he delivered with such love and joy that it made every moment with him a memorable experience. He was a joyous man who had natural leadership skills with any group, and his charisma made people both love and follow him.

His personality always made him the center of attention, even coming close to obscuring how great a football player he was. With a combination of speed, power, and instinct, Brown was the kind of player who could penetrate the gaps, get to the ball carrier, harass quarterbacks, and generally mess up a game plan. It's one thing to be a leader on a team that consists of average players, but it's quite another when your teammates include Reggie White, Clyde Simmons, Seth Joyner, and Wes Hopkins. These were big-time stars who looked to Brown to keep them loose, fired up, and at the top of their game—and he did, without fail.

Ryan loved Brown's all-out enthusiasm and the impact that he had on his teammates. "Jerome was the one who got the defense started," Ryan said. "He was the leader of that group, and they all followed him."

Reggie White holds up the retired jersey No. 99 of fallen teammate Jerome Brown during a September 1992 dedication ceremony.

And how that group could play! Like Ryan's previous defense in Chicago, the Eagles played with fire, tenacity, anger, and intelligence. They were on the field to win, but they were there to punish as well. Their swagger came from their knowledge that they were a unique group with talent and ability to spare, and Brown gave the unit most of its personality. "This is the kind of guy that will take you places, take you to the big game," Ryan said. "He had attitude and he backed it up with every step he took and every move he made."

Brown enjoyed the team's twice yearly competitions with division rivals like the Giants, Cowboys, and Redskins, and he always tried to exact an emotional edge in those games. He told the Giants offensive linemen that they should bring some kind of weapons with them if they wanted to slow down the Eagles pass rush. "You better bring something with you," Brown said. "You're dealing with Jerome Brown and Reggie White." Brown knew that White gave the Eagles a formidable presence on the field.

Mike Golic is known as the host of the *Mike and Mike* radio program, the cornerstone of ESPN's radio lineup, to a generation of fans. But before his broadcasting career he was a bruising tackle who lined up next to Brown and believed there was nothing phony about his teammate, whether he was laughing or scrapping.

"I never knew anyone like him, but who did?" Golic said. "He was about the most unique guy I ever came across."

Brown was the kind of player that either loved you or hated you right from the get-go. There was no middle ground. He was also unwilling to take it easy in the late stages of a blowout victory or in so-called exhibition games like the Pro Bowl. In fact, the last game he ever played in was the Pro Bowl following the 1991 season. In a contest in which most of the players are more interested in chartering fishing boats and making dinner reservations, Brown got into separate scuffles with Houston guard Bruce Matthews and Raiders guard Steve Wisniewski. He didn't apologize for causing a ruckus, either. Whether it was with his own teammates in the heat of training camp or the nastiest guy in the league (which Wisniewski was), Brown was a ball of fire.

"That was Jerome," said Golic. "He wouldn't hesitate to go if he had the inclination. But when it was over, it was over. He did not hold any grudges.

"My best memories of him off the field are the meetings we would have on Friday or Saturday morning after Jerome had been out the night before. You would hear what he did, or just the way he would describe it, and you had to laugh. He would make you laugh every other minute."

Brown's energy level was what separated him from other interior defensive tackles. At 6'2" and about 300 pounds, he did not necessarily look like a brilliant athlete. He constantly battled his weight. But on the football field, lined up in a three-point stance, he was a revving engine waiting for the snap so he could fire. The quickness in his initial jump was shocking to even the most experienced offensive linemen.

Diplomacy was not the name of Brown's game, either. The Eagles were selected to play in the American Bowl in London prior to the 1989 season, and Brown had no problem with crossing the Atlantic and playing in England. But once there, he was not enamored with many of the British ways of doing things that he came across, and he was not shy about letting the press know. He had problems with the hygiene in England. When he went to a popular nightclub, the aroma was quite pungent. "It was bad out there," Brown said of the smell on the dance floor. "I didn't know those people didn't use deodorant. Whew!"

Brown told it like it was. He also played the game as if there was no tomorrow—though he did not practice that way. He was always battling nagging injuries, so he often missed practice because of knee and shoulder problems. But he never missed a game.

While Ryan loved Brown's honesty and ferocity, Eagles owner Norman Braman was not such a big fan. He thought Brown had a big mouth and was crude and rude. He was embarrassed by the Eagles' image as a bunch of nasty boys. Braman either never noticed or didn't care that Brown played his heart out. He let it become known that he had little patience for his leadership.

"That really hurt Jerome," said Ryan. "What did he expect from the guy? Jerome was a great player who laid it on the line—and he did it for them. He was there on Sunday. Some days he was great and others he was not. But nobody ever played harder than Jerome."

While the criticism hurt Brown—although he would never acknowledge it publicly—he did take a look at himself in the mirror and decided that he could do more to prepare for the season. Instead of eating everything he loved, Brown hired a nutritionist to prepare a menu of healthy foods for him. Did Jerome ever cheat on his diet? Of course. But he stuck to it as best he could, and he worked out diligently.

His primary workout partner prior to the start of the 1991 season was Cortez Kennedy, a rookie defensive tackle who had just been drafted out of the University of Miami by the Seattle Seahawks. Kennedy was an outstanding player with a body type similar to Brown's. They worked out hard and pushed each other.

"That's when we became close friends," Kennedy told journalist Phil Anastasia in his book on the Eagles entitled *Broken Wing, Broken Promise.* "We lived together. We did everything together. We rode jet skis. We had a great time just trying to get in shape. We would eat light for a couple of days and then say, 'Forget it.'

"We had eaten one of the nutritionist's meals one day. We came in at about 1:00 AM and a friend brought some chicken over. I caught Jerome eating the chicken and asked him what he was doing. I chased him around the house and he was chewing it and spitting it out...and laughing. We had good times like that."

His teammates took notice of his improved efforts before the 1991 season. Not only was he more serious in the weight room, but there was a change in his mind-set. He no longer said everything that popped into his head. He still had fun, but he saw less reason to entertain everyone at every moment.

Brown, who had made the Pro Bowl at the end of the 1990 season, signed a new contract prior to the 1991 season opener. His three-year, $3.3 million deal may seem tiny by today's standards, but it made Brown a happy man—and a very motivated player.

He told head coach Richie Kotite that the defense was going to have an awesome year, and it did just that. The Eagles were number one in the league against the run and the pass, and in total defense. They finished with a 10–6 record despite losing quarterback Randall Cunningham to an injury on the second play of the season. The only thing that kept the Eagles out of the postseason was the NFL's tiebreaker system. They had one fewer NFC win than the Atlanta Falcons, so they just missed making the playoffs.

Brown had a remarkable season, recording nine sacks from his interior line position. He also made big plays at key moments and thoroughly impressed new defensive coordinator Bud Carson with both his play and his demeanor. "On game day, you could just see that he wanted to be there and that he hated to lose," Carson said. "This was 100 percent genuine.

That attitude rubbed off on everybody else around him."

As he prepared for the 1992 season, life was good for Brown. He was in great shape a few weeks before the start of training camp, and he was looking forward to a huge season with the Eagles. The team would also have a healthy Cunningham on board again and had signed running back Herschel Walker to shore up their running game.

But in late June, Brown lost control of the sports car he was driving shortly after a midday rain left the road he was on somewhat slick. Driving with his 12-year-old nephew in the car, Brown crashed into a utility pole, killing them both.

An immediate police investigation ruled out the possibility that Brown had been impaired by drugs or alcohol. "He accelerated rapidly, went into an erratic slide pattern, and slid off the road," said Brooksville, Florida, captain Ray Schumacher. "There was no sign of impaired driving. There was nothing to suggest that. We do not know what caused the accident."

Brown's family, friends, and teammates went into complete shock. As word of the tragedy spread among his teammates, the shock and grief were overwhelming. When Golic told fellow Eagles player Clyde Simmons what had happened, Simmons was unable to speak. Joyner, viewed by many as the toughest and perhaps meanest player in the game, broke down and cried as he attempted to relay the news to teammates.

Nobody took it harder than White. The great defensive end was preparing to speak at the Billy Graham Crusade when the phone call came in. "I put down the phone and cried. He was like my younger brother and now he was gone."

Kotite, who regularly struggled with his ability to verbalize the problems faced by his football team, was at his best in this team crisis. He understood what Brown had meant to the team both on and off the field. "When you were around Jerome, you always felt he was indestructible," Kotite said. "You just had that feeling. But his life got snuffed out, and that is really hard to deal with."

Golic says that Brown's impact on his life is a constant, even though the accident took him away so many years ago. "I can honestly say that there's not any significant period of time that I don't think about Jerome," Golic said. "He was just such an original, with not one phony bone in him. He liked to have fun. He liked to play. He liked being one of the guys. Nobody was ever a better teammate. You just can't duplicate what he brought to the team."

Less than two weeks after their teammate's death, the Eagles opened training camp in West Chester, Pennsylvania. Nobody was really ready to begin the season, but the NFL calendar waits for no team. They practiced and played with a heavy heart, but in the end they proved themselves to be warriors who gave their all despite the sadness they all shared. Isn't that what Brown would have wanted?

The Eagles memorialized Brown by leaving his locker undisturbed for the 1992 season. "We weren't going to put anybody in his locker this year, so I thought [the] idea was great," Kotite said. "He was a big part of this football team, and I don't ever want them to forget that." The nameplate "BROWN" stayed up all year, along with his turf shoes, grass cleats, and socks. A hard hat and a floppy rain hat served as constant reminders of their fallen leader.

The Eagles went on to an 11–5 season and a spot in the playoffs as a wild-card team while wearing their emotions on their sleeves. They earned a memorable 36–20 wild-card win over New Orleans in the Superdome before losing to the Cowboys in the divisional playoffs.

Brown would not have liked the way the season ended, but a road win in the playoffs would have put a smile on the big man's face that would have lit up the city.

LORD, I WAS BORN A GAMBLING MAN

Making money in the NFL should be easy. Teams are guaranteed to take in more from television revenues than they pay out in salaries. And that's not even counting ticket sales and revenues from NFL Properties. Professional football is a substantial industry that turns a monstrous profit.

But when an owner like Leonard Tose gets involved, nothing is guaranteed. Tose was welcomed like a conquering hero when he bought the team for $16.1 million in 1969 from the crumbling

Jerry Wolman, who was forced to sell the team by bankruptcy court officials.

The sale price was the highest ever for a U.S.-based sports franchise at the time, but Tose seemed able to afford it. He clearly had a distinctive style and a passion for high living, including owning his own jet, smoking expensive cigars, and dining at exclusive restaurants just about every night. His regular pose was with a Scotch in one hand and a cigarette in the other.

He also had an eye for the ladies and was eventually married five times. He made a habit of giving his wives extraordinary baubles and gifts. For example, he bought his fourth wife a matching set of Rolls Royces that the two delighted in driving at the same time.

Tose was a charmer who had money and vices to go along with it. He was an exciting individual to follow around, something akin to a Damon Runyon character come to life. But Tose's compulsive personality was fraught with problems, the most damaging of which was a lifelong addiction to gambling.

His gambling problems first came to light a few years after he bought the Eagles, during divorce proceedings from his third wife, Andrea. In her divorce complaint she stated that Tose "habitually and compulsively engages in illegal and incompetent gambling, incurring losses of very large sums of money."

Andrea's statement was by no means the only allegation concerning Tose's gambling issues. Jack Anderson, one of the nation's most popular syndicated columnists during the 1960s and '70s, wrote that Tose wagered "fabulous sums" on gin rummy and golf.

Compulsive gambling is a progressive illness. In the end, it nearly cost Philadelphia its beloved team. But during his tenure as owner, Tose also made several significant contributions to the Eagles. The most important of these was the hiring of Dick Vermeil as head coach in 1976. Vermeil was able to change the Eagles' culture of losing through his hard work, keen eye for talent, determination, and charisma.

That charisma caught Tose's eye when he watched Vermeil coach UCLA to a Rose Bowl upset over powerful Ohio State on January 1, 1976. Tose could sense the energy that Vermeil projected to his players and realized that perhaps that was the key ingredient that his team was missing. Tose had fired Mike McCormack after a 4–10 season in 1975; he then set his cap on Vermeil and got him. The Eagles had endured 13 losing seasons during their last 14 years, and Tose was desperate to turn that streak around—even if it meant hiring an untested 36-year-old college boy as head coach.

Tose's foresight was rewarded following the 1980 season when the Eagles' made their first Super Bowl appearance, and the team's first appearance in a championship game since 1960. Tose partied and celebrated during every night of Super Bowl week in New Orleans, and he was supremely disappointed when the Eagles lost to the Raiders.

In addition to giving Vermeil his big break, Tose let the people he hired do their jobs with little interference on his part. "Was Leonard involved with the team?" said Vermeil. "Of course he was. He loved the team. But did he want us to go after certain players or run plays that he thought would work? Never. The only question he ever asked was, 'What can I do to help you do your job?' He was a great man to work for and he was very kind."

Tose was also admired by many of the players—and that's a rarity in the NFL. "He never claimed to be God's gift to the football world, but he was the best supporting person you could imagine," said former Eagles linebacker Bill Bergey. "All the players loved him."

Tose loved to spend money in a showy fashion and always seemed to need to prove that he was a "big shot." His tendency to flaunt his wealth turned a lot of people off, but he was also incredibly charitable. His donations to Philadelphia's public school system to help keep their extracurricular activities afloat were just one example. He also bought bulletproof vests for the Philadelphia police department and gave huge sums of money to the Ronald McDonald House and to cancer research. The bone-marrow transplant laboratory at Philadelphia's Children's Hospital was dedicated to Tose and the Eagles as a result of his many contributions.

He also helped out many needy individuals with heartfelt gifts and took care of his employees and friends with generous rewards as well. That included Vermeil, who would remain loyal to Tose throughout the remainder of the owner's life—even after his gambling changed him into a pitiful shell of his former self.

Gambling and excessive spending led to a mountain of debt that changed Tose's personality. Some time around the 1982 strike he became overwhelmed by his losses, and he took it out on his players and his team. Those close to him knew that he was unhappy and that he was just venting his frustrations.

"He was depressed," Vermeil told legendary Philadelphia newspaperman Ray Didinger in his extensive book *The Eagles Encyclopedia*. "He was under so much stress at that time, he said things I know he didn't mean. That was the most depressed I've ever seen him," said Vermeil.

Tose fired longtime Eagles general manager Jimmy Murray and replaced him with his daughter, Susan Tose Fletcher. But this was no case of nepotism. Tose needed his daughter to get rid of the red ink in which he was drowning. Her job was to do anything possible to right the financial ship.

In 1984 her mission almost sent the Eagles to Arizona. Real estate executive James Monaghan offered to buy 25 percent of the team if Tose would agree to move it to Arizona. The deal would have allowed Tose to maintain control of the team while also getting rid of his debt.

If the Eagles had been a furniture store, nobody would have cared. But an NFL franchise is a status symbol for major American cities, and its importance to the fans simply cannot be quantified. Philadelphia mayor Wilson Goode stepped in and made some promises to Tose regarding skyboxes and the team's lease at Veterans Stadium. While it didn't come close to what Tose was being offered to move the team to the desert, he knew in his heart that he could never really move the team away from the city that loved it so dearly.

Cleveland Browns fans can only wish that their former owner, the selfish Art Modell, had had one iota of the conscience that Tose had when it came time to do the right thing. Modell, of course, moved the Browns from Cleveland to Baltimore, where they became the Ravens, following the 1995 season. Cleveland was without a team until the league decided to undo Modell's egregious wrong by expanding back to the city on the shores of Lake Erie in 1999.

In 1985 Tose was forced to sell the Eagles to Norman Braman for $65 million. He could have enjoyed a very comfortable retirement, but he lost nearly all of the $10 million he had realized from the sale of the team on gambling. Tose even filed suit against one of the Atlantic City casinos, saying that they had given him excessive amounts of alcohol so he would lose all semblance of control and gamble away his money.

He never had a chance at winning that lawsuit. Nor did he have a chance in the casinos, where he lost habitually at blackjack and roulette. Tose once lost more than $1 million in a single night and estimated his lifetime gambling losses at $40 to $50 million. The gambling clearly had disastrous effects on his life. He was evicted from his home in Philadelphia on his 81st birthday and ended up living in a hotel room until he died in 2003 at the age of 88.

Vermeil never forgot what his old boss had done for him. He stayed in touch with Tose until his death and gave him money whenever it was needed.

Tose never got help for his problem. Either too proud, too stubborn, or (most likely) too embarrassed, he never made any real attempt to stop gambling, either through counseling or by attending Gamblers Anonymous meetings. In the end, his legacy as a beaten, frustrated loser outstripped what he had done with the rest of his life.

Gambling destroyed Leonard Tose's life, and it also nearly cost the city its beloved team.

WORST. TRADE. EVER.

The Eagles went through many dark years before Vermeil brought the team back into prominence in the late 1970s. The last championship, of course, was the 1960 title, earned with a 17–10 victory over Vince Lombardi's Green Bay Packers. It was the only postseason defeat Lombardi's team ever suffered.

The Eagles were a very solid 10–4 in 1961, but fell to second place in the Eastern Conference behind a New York Giants team that was 10–3–1. New York may actually have saved the Eagles some embarrassment by winning the conference title, since the Giants wound up facing a superior Green Bay team and absorbing a 37–0 beating.

The Eagles fell on hard times in 1962 and '63, finishing in last place both years, and the team felt the need to make a change. They decided to shake things up by trading for quarterback Norm Snead and cornerback Claude Crabb of the Washington Redskins.

If the Eagles had traded a draft pick, or perhaps any other player on their roster, the trade would no longer even be remembered. But the Eagles traded one of the best pure passers ever to play the game: Christian Adolph Jurgensen, better known as Sonny.

The trade had an impact on both teams. It helped propel the Redskins toward the top of the NFL. Although it would take a few more years and many moves to get there, having perhaps the game's smoothest passer certainly helped their transition from stumblebums to contenders.

Back in Philly, the trade rooted the Eagles to the bottom of the league. They managed a 9–5 season in 1966, but that was their only winning year following the trade until 1978.

The Eagles made the trade on April 1, 1964, at the behest of new head coach Joe Kuharich. Jurgensen, who grew up in Wilmington, North Carolina, played his college football at Duke University and was drafted by Philadelphia in the fourth round in 1957. He had performed very well for the Eagles in 1961, the year after Norm Van Brocklin retired. He led the league with 32 touchdown passes, throwing for 3,723 yards. But when the team fell on hard times in 1962 and '63, Jurgensen was blamed.

Kuharich, who would make a slew of bad decisions during his five-year "reign of error" from 1964 to 1968, had a difficult personality and was reviled by the press. But the way the media portrayed him was by no means unfair. The Jurgensen trade was not his only big-time bumble; he also traded Irv Cross, Tommy McDonald, and Maxie Baughan. When it came to judging talent in the draft, Kuharich picked such mediocre players as offensive tackle Ray

The Eagles trade of Sonny Jurgensen to the Redskins in 1964 ranks among
the worst in the history of the NFL.

Rissmiller from the University of Georgia in the second round in
1965 and defensive end Randy Beisler of Indiana University in the
first round of the 1966 pick (4th overall). It was no better in 1967,
when the Eagles selected running back Harry Jones from the
University of Arkansas with their first round pick (19th overall).

Perhaps the only thing worse than Kuharich's decisions with

the Eagles were those of his boss, owner Wolman. Before the end of Kuharich's first season, Wolman gave the embattled head coach an unheard of 15-year extension on his contract. "I feel with the personnel changes Joe has made and with the leadership he has provided, he has the team moving in the right direction," Wolman said.

Eagles fans couldn't be sure what was coming, but they had a pretty good idea that disaster was around the corner—and they were right.

The Jurgensen trade made no sense from the beginning. While Snead had size and a strong arm, Jurgensen had astounding accuracy with his passes and a very strong arm himself. Though he was not a huge man—6'0" and 203 pounds—he had a gift for throwing the ball and could wing it 80 yards if pressed to do so. While he had a bit of a sidearm delivery and a punch above the belt, he was one of the most consistently "catchable" quarterbacks in NFL history. Even though he didn't have the same kind of numbers as Baltimore's Johnny Unitas, Green Bay's Bart Starr, and the New York Jets' Joe Namath, Jurgensen is considered their equal, or perhaps even their superior, when it came to putting the ball where he wanted it.

How did Jurgensen himself feel about the trade? "I was shocked in a way," he said. "I had just met with the new coach [Kuharich] of the Eagles, who had come in with the new owner [Wolman]. I met with him, sat in his office for a few hours, talked about what we were going to do, what offense we were going to have, and how we were going to win again.

"I left, went to lunch, met some friends of mine. Then someone came in and said, 'You were traded to the Redskins.' I said, 'No, it's April Fool's Day. You're kidding.' He said, 'No, I'm not kidding. I just heard it on the radio.' So I was shocked.

"When I looked back on it, being shocked initially, it was an opportunity to start fresh and to start anew. It [the Redskins] was a team I had followed, because the Redskins were part of the South. I had come up to see them play when I was in high school. My family could come up and see me play. I enjoyed that."

Jurgensen would go on to play for 18 seasons in the NFL; he

was a five-time Pro Bowl selection and earned three NFL individual passing titles. He was elected to the Hall of Fame in 1983.

Former Redskins receiver Charlie Taylor described Jurgensen as an instinctive thrower who made the game easier for the players around him. "The NFL back then had other great quarterbacks, like Unitas and Starr," Taylor said. "But Sonny was the guy when it came to pure passing. He had a feel for the game, a feel for what was happening. He made things easier for you."

Both Snead and Crabb—the players Jurgensen was traded for—turned out to be solid performers for the Eagles, but neither could come close to matching Jurgensen's impact. During his 18-year NFL career Snead, a native of the Newport News, Virginia, area who was drafted in round 1 by the Redskins in 1961, played for five NFL teams—Washington, Philadelphia, Minnesota, the New York Giants, and San Francisco. Crabb played for seven years—with the Redskins, the Eagles, and the Los Angeles Rams—before retiring in 1968.

It was perhaps the best trade ever by the Redskins—and the worst ever for the Eagles.

SOURCES

Books

Barra, Allen. *Big Play: Barra on Football*. Dulles, VA: Potomac Books, 2004

Benedict, Jeff and Don Yaeger. *Pros and Cons: The Criminals Who Play in the NFL*. New York: Grand Central Publishing, 1999

Bennett, Tom. The Pro Style: The Complete Guide to Understanding National Football League Strategy. Prentice-Hall, 1976

Carroll, Bob et al. *Total Football II*. New York: HarperCollins, 1999

Daly, Dan and Bob O'Donnell. *The Pro Football Chronicle*. McMillan, 1990

Davis, Jeff. *Papa Bear*. New York: McGraw-Hill, 2006

Dawson, Len. Inside Quarterbacking. Regnery, 1972

Didinger, Ray. *Game Plans for Success*. New York: McGraw-Hill, 1996

Didinger, Ray and Robert Lyons. *The Eagles Encyclopedia*. Philadelphia: Temple University Press, 2005

Forbes, Gordon. *Tales from the Eagles Sidelines*. Champaign, IL: Sports Publishing Inc., 2006

King, Peter. *Inside the Helmet*. New York: Simon & Schuster, 1993

Klemash, Christian. *How to Succeed in the Game of Life: 34 Interviews with the World's Greatest Coaches*. Kansas City, MO: Andrews McMeel, 2006

Liebman, Glen. *Sports Shorts*. Chicago: McGraw-Hill/Contemporary, 1993

MacCambridge, Michael. *America's Game*. New York: Random House, 2004

Moldea, Dan E. *Interference: How Organized Crime Influences Professional Football*. New York: William Morrow & Co., 1995

National Football League. *2007 NFL Record and Fact Book*

Parcell, Bill and Mike Lupica. *Parcells: Autobiography of the Biggest Giant of Them All*. Bonus Books, 1987

Philadelphia Eagles. *Media Guide*, 2007

Plimpton, George. One *More July*. New York: Berkley, 1978

Weiss, Don and Chuck Day. *The Making of the Super Bowl*. New York: McGraw-Hill, 2003

White, Reggie and Terry Hill. *Reggie White, Minister of Defense*. Brentwood, TN: Wolgemuth & Hyatt, 1991

Zimmerman, Paul. *A Thinking Man's Guide to Pro Football*. Dutton, 1971

Periodicals and newspapers

Chicago Tribune
The Dallas Morning News
The (Newark) *Star-Ledger*
Philadelphia Daily News
The Philadelphia Inquirer
Pittsburgh Post-Gazette
Pro Football Weekly
The Sporting News
Sports Illustrated
The Washington Post

Websites

Coldhardfootballfacts.com
Eaglefan.com
ESPN.com
InsidetheEagles.com
NFL.com
NJ.com
PhiladelphiaEagles.com
Phillyburbs.com